my revision notes

AQA AS/A-level History

STUART BRITAIN AND THE CRISIS OF MONARCHY

1603–1702

Oliver Bullock

Series editor
David Ferriby

HODDER EDUCATION
AN HACHETTE UK COMPANY

Orders: please contact Hachette UK Distribution, Hely Hutchinson Centre, Milton Road, Didcot, Oxfordshire, OX11 7HH. Telephone: +44 (0)1235 827827. Email education@hachette.co.uk Lines are open from 9 a.m. to 5 p.m., Monday to Friday. You can also order through our website: www.hoddereducation.co.uk

ISBN: 978 1 5104 1803 5

© Oliver Bullock 2018

First published in 2018 by
Hodder Education,
An Hachette UK Company
Carmelite House
50 Victoria Embankment
London EC4Y 0DZ

www.hoddereducation.co.uk

The authorised representative in the EEA is Hachette Ireland, 8 Castlecourt Centre, Dublin 15, D15 XTP3, Ireland (email: info@hbgi.ie)

Impression number   10 9 8 7 6 5

Year   2022

Cover photo © Shutterstock/Demisteriman
Illustrations by Integra
Typeset by Integra Software Services Pvt. Ltd., Pondicherry, India
Printed and bound by CPI Group (UK) Ltd, Croydon CR0 4YY

A catalogue record for this title is available from the British Library.

My revision planner

Part 2: Monarchy restored and restrained: Britain, 1649–1702 (A-level only)

Introduction

Component 1: Breadth study

Component 1 involves the study of significant developments over an extended period of time (around 50 years at AS and 100 years at A-level) and an evaluation of historical interpretations.

Stuart Britain and the crisis of monarchy, 1603–1702

The specification lists the content of Stuart Britain and the crisis of monarchy, 1603–1702, in two parts, each part being divided into two sections.

Part 1:

- Absolutism challenged: Britain, 1603–49
- Monarchs and Parliaments, 1603–29
- Revolution, 1629–49

Part 2:

- Monarchy restored and restrained: Britain, 1649–1702 (A-level only)
- From republic to restored and limited monarchy, 1649–78
- The establishment of constitutional monarchy, 1678–1702

Although each period of study is set out in chronological sections in the specification, an exam question may arise from one or more of these sections.

The AS examination which you may be taking includes all the content in Part 1.

You are required to answer:

- Section A: one question on two contrasting interpretations – which is the more convincing? You need to identify the arguments in each extract and assess how convincing they are, using your knowledge, and then reach a judgement on which is the more convincing. The question is worth 25 marks.
- Section B: one essay question out of two. The questions will be set on a broad topic reflecting that this is a breadth paper, and will require you to analyse whether you agree or disagree with a statement. Almost certainly, you will be doing both and reaching a balanced conclusion. The question is worth 25 marks.

The exam lasts one and a half hours, and you should spend about equal time on each section.

At AS-level, Component 1 will be worth a total of 50 marks and 50% of the AS examination.

The A-level examination at the end of the course includes all the content of both parts.

You are required to answer:

- Section A: one question on three interpretations – how convincing is each interpretation? You are NOT required to reach a conclusion about which might be the most convincing. You need to identify the arguments in each extract and use your knowledge to assess how convincing each one is. The question is worth 30 marks.
- Section B: two essay questions out of three. The questions will be set on a broad topic (usually covering 20–25 years). The question-styles will vary but they will all require you to analyse factors and reach a conclusion. The focus may be on causation, or consequence, or continuity and change. Each question in this section is worth 25 marks.

The exam lasts for two and a half hours. You should spend about one hour on Section A and about 45 minutes on each of the two essays.

At A-level, Component 1 will be worth a total of 80 marks and 40% of the A-level examination.

In both the AS and A-level examinations you are being tested on the ability to:

- use relevant historical information (Sections A and B)
- evaluate different historical interpretations (Section A)
- the skill of analysing factors and reaching a judgement (Section B)

How to use this book

This book has been designed to help you develop the knowledge and skills necessary to succeed in the examination.

- The book is divided into four sections – one for each section of the A-level specification.
- Each section is made up of a series of topics organised into double-page spreads.
- On the left-hand page you will find a summary of the key content you will need to learn.
- Words in bold in the key content are defined in the Glossary (see pages 90–91).
- On the right-hand page you will find exam-focused activities.

Together these two strands of the book will provide you with the knowledge and skills essential for examination success.

▼ Key historical content

▼ Exam-focused activities

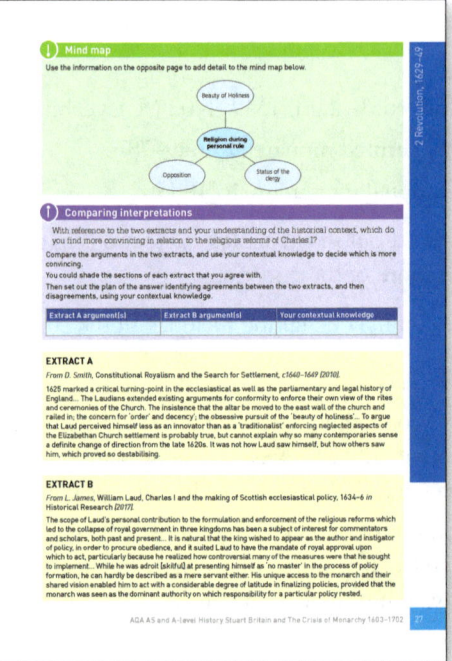

Examination activities

There are three levels of exam focused activities:

- Band 1 activities are designed to develop the foundation skills needed to pass the exam. These have a green heading and this symbol
- Band 2 activities are designed to build on the skills developed in Band 1 activities and to help you to achieve a C grade. These have an orange heading and this symbol
- Band 3 activities are designed to enable you to access the highest grades. These have a purple heading and this symbol
- Some of the activities have answers or suggested answers which can be found online. These have the following symbol to indicate this

Each section ends with an exam-style question and sample answers with commentary. This will give you guidance on what is expected to achieve the top grade.

You can also keep track of your revision by ticking off each topic heading in the book, or by ticking the checklist on the contents page. Tick each box when you have:

- revised and understood a topic
- completed the activities.

Mark schemes

For some of the activities in the book it will be useful to refer to the mark schemes for this paper. Below are abbreviated forms.

Section A – Interpretations

Level	AS-level exam	A-level exam
1	Unsupported vague or general comments. Little understanding of the interpretations. (1–5)	Mostly general or vague comments. OR shows an accurate understanding of one extract only. (1–6)
2	Partial understanding of the interpretations. Undeveloped comments with a little knowledge. (6–10)	Some accurate comments on interpretations given in at least two of the extracts. Some analysis, but little evaluation. (7–12)
3	Reasonable understanding of interpretations. Some knowledge to support arguments. (11–15)	Some supported comments on the three interpretations with comments on strength, with some analysis and evaluation. (13–18)
4	Good understanding of interpretations. A supported conclusion, but not all comments well-substantiated and judgements may be limited. (16–20)	Good understanding of the interpretations, combined with knowledge of historical context, with mostly well-supported evaluation, but with minor limitations in depth and breadth. (19–24)
5	Good understanding of interpretations. Thorough evaluation of extracts leading to a well-substantiated judgement. (21–25)	Very good understanding of interpretations, combined with strong awareness of historical context to analyse and evaluate with well-supported arguments. (25–30)

Section B – Essays

Level	AS-level exam	A-level exam
1	Extremely limited or irrelevant information. Unsupported vague or generalist comments. (1–5)	Extremely limited or irrelevant information. Unsupported vague or generalist comments. (1–5)
2	Descriptive or partial, failing to grasp full demands of question. Limited in scope. (6–10)	Descriptive or partial, failing to grasp full demands of question. Limited in scope. (6–10)
3	Some understanding and answer is adequately organised. Information showing understanding of some key features. (11–15)	Understanding of question and a range of largely accurate information showing awareness of key issues and features, but lacking in precise detail. Some balance established. (11–15)
4	Understanding shown with range of largely accurate information showing awareness of some of key issues and features. (16–20)	Good understanding of question. Well-organised and effectively communicated with range of clear and specific supporting information showing good understanding of key features and issues, with some conceptual awareness. (16–20)
5	Good understanding. Well-organised and effectively communicated. Range of clear information showing good understanding and some conceptual awareness leading to a substantiated judgement. (21–25)	Very good understanding of full demands of question. Well-organised and effectively delivered, with well-selected precise supporting information. Fully analytical with balanced argument and well-substantiated judgement. (21–25)

1 Monarchs and Parliaments, 1603–29

The Political Nation, the social basis of power and James I

The Monarch

In the seventeenth century, the monarch was the most important individual in the political system. There was no true democracy in the form that we would understand it today. The prerogative powers possessed by monarchs enabled them to control the following areas of government:

- They could declare war.
- They could sign treaties with foreign powers.
- They had the power to call Parliament when they wished (and dissolve it).
- They could appoint a Privy Council of their own choosing for the day-to-day running of government.
- They controlled some sources of income such as money received from feudal dues and customs duties.

Despite these powers, the monarch faced restrictions:

- In order to pass legislation, a Parliament had to be called. This meant that Members of Parliament (MPs) could scrutinise and debate proposed laws. This could lead to conflict and division.
- Normal Crown revenue was often not enough for a monarch, especially in times of war. This meant that Parliament was relied upon to approve new taxes. If Parliament did not agree to a tax, a political stalemate could occur.

The Political Nation

The Political Nation was composed of those people who were able to become involved in political activity at both a national and local level. This group essentially consisted of the nobility and gentry, some professionals such as lawyers, as well as wealthy merchants who were normally based in London. The group formed no more than 1 per cent of the total population.

The social basis of power

The power of the Political Nation was based on a number of factors:

- There was a property qualification of approximately £2 per year in order to vote. This meant that there was no danger of power being shared with the lower classes.

- Members of the Political Nation carried out national roles in politics, such as becoming members of the Privy Council and MPs.
- Wealth – and therefore power – was primarily based on land ownership. Enclosure, which developed briskly in the preceding century, meant that some large landowners were able to increase their wealth further.
- As urbanisation increased (London overtook Paris and Naples to become the largest city in Western Europe around 1640), the wealth of merchants – and those in associated professions such as banking and insurance – increased. London was on the path to becoming the centre of an empire that controlled colonies in North America and the Caribbean, and those that benefited financially from London's growth were able to join the Political Nation.

James I

Character

James came to the throne in England in 1603 after becoming James VI of Scotland in 1566. His mother, Mary Queen of Scots, was a cousin of the childless Elizabeth I, making James the closest heir. James's character can be summed up as follows:

- He was intelligent, and was the author of a number of books, including a guide to hunting witches entitled *Daemonologie* in 1597.
- Eight months after his birth, James's father, Lord Darnley, was murdered. This, along with his own mother's execution following Catholic plots against Elizabeth I, contributed to a lifelong fear of threats to his throne.
- He had a thorough education and his tutors schooled him in Presbyterian doctrine.
- As well as his intelligence, he was also vain and shallow, and spent huge sums of money on clothes and artwork.
- He was extremely trusting of his Scottish advisers and had a string of royal favourites.

Views of monarchy

James believed strongly in the **Divine Right of Kings** and published a work entitled *The True Law of Free Monarchies* in 1598. In this work he made a number of claims:

- He stated that God places kings on the throne and that monarchs should be able to wield unrestrained power.

- Kings are able to act above the law and are not subject to normal judicial procedures.

- In common with most other monarchs in the early modern period, he saw Parliament as something that served him when he required, rather than a core element of the political system.

 Mind map

Use the information on the opposite page to add detail to the mind map below.

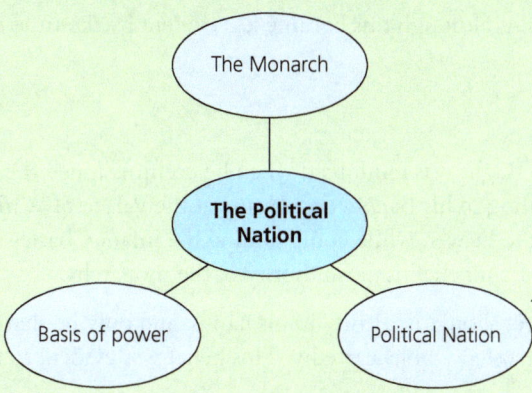

 Introducing an argument

Below is an essay-style question. Look at the two introductions and decide which is the more effective. Could either be improved – especially in relation to Level 5 answers?

'The power of the monarchy was unrivalled in the early seventeenth century'. Assess the validity of this view.

Introduction 1

There is much evidence to suggest that the power of the monarchy was unrivalled in the early seventeenth century. The monarch possessed a number of prerogative powers and this meant that he was able to appoint his own advisers, decide on matters of war and peace and call Parliament at any time. Despite this power, the Political Nation was able to hold some influence over the monarchy. MPs could delay subsidies or grants of new taxes if they were dissatisfied with a monarch and, as the gentry were becoming wealthier in the century, they inevitably became more powerful. It is clear, however, that the amount of power wielded depended on the individual monarch, and as James believed strongly in Divine Right he was prepared to rule without parliament for long periods of time.

Introduction 2

Monarchs were extremely powerful in the seventeenth century. They were able to call and dismiss Parliament whenever they wanted and sign treaties with foreign powers. They were also able to control some taxes which meant that they could become very rich. The money from these taxes was often used to fight foreign wars and pay royal favourites and courtiers. James was a particularly powerful monarch because he believed strongly in Divine Right.

Charles I: character and views on monarchy

Character

Charles I was born in 1600 and in 1612 his older brother, Henry, died unexpectedly. This left Charles as the heir to the throne. Charles had spent much of his childhood away from the royal court and was underprepared for this role. His character was shaped by these early experiences.

- He was a poor public speaker and suffered from a stammer.
- He disapproved of his father's extravagance at court and favoured an orderly, hierarchical approach to government.
- One important trait that he did inherit from his father was a firm belief in the Divine Right of Kings.
- As a young man he angered easily, although this became less evident by the time he became king in 1625.

Views of monarchy

Charles's firm belief in the Divine Right was reinforced when he commissioned the Dutch artist Peter Paul Rubens to paint the ceiling of his Banqueting House at the Palace of Whitehall. The painting depicts James I ascending to heaven while commanding the infant Charles to the throne. This represented the Stuart kings' firm belief in the authority of the monarchy.

Charles believed that political power should lie firmly in his hands, and only be shared with a select number of advisers who he trusted wholeheartedly. This belief was evident in the reforms he made to the royal court.

- Ceremonies surrounding visits to the king modelled on those exercised in France were introduced.
- Unlike his father, Charles made himself difficult to access and viewed outsiders with suspicion.
- A sense of ritual was brought into the court and Charles was served food on bended knee.
- He appointed Arminian chaplains who believed strongly in Divine Right.
- His fondness for ceremony and hierarchy was reflected in his preference for Arminian-style worship, and his Arminian advisers were held in high regard.

Aims

Charles's aims as king can be summarised as follows:

- Restore a sense of order and decorum to the royal court.
- Maintain order in the Church.
- Establish a sound financial base, in response to debts created by his father's rule.
- Secure the authority of the monarchy.
- Maintain a firm control over his three kingdoms of England, Ireland and Scotland. This meant balancing their conflicting religious and cultural differences.

Favourites

Like his father, Charles caused controversy by deferring to his favourites in order to make important decisions. His tendency to place complete trust in his close advisers made Parliament suspicious of him and later he was compelled to choose advisers who were acceptable to his legislature.

! Delete as applicable

Below is a sample essay question and a paragraph written in answer to this question. Read the paragraph and decide which option (in bold) is the most appropriate. Delete the less appropriate options and complete the paragraph by justifying your selection.

To what extent was the character of Charles I responsible for the weaknesses of the Stuart monarchy before 1629?

The character of Charles I was **the most important reason/an important reason/just one of many reasons** why the Stuart monarchy faced problems before 1629. Charles was obsessed with order and hierarchy which reflected his firm belief in Divine Right and his keen interest in Arminianism. He promoted Arminian clergy which resulted in opposition from the Political Nation. This opposition **was in direct response to/was partly in response to/was connected** with Charles's character.

_____

_____

_____

_____

_____

! Interpretation: content or argument?   a

Read the following interpretation on the character of Charles I and the two alternative answers to the question. Which answer focuses more on the content and which focuses more on the arguments of the interpretation? Explain your answer.

With reference to your understanding of the historical context, assess how convincing the arguments in this extract are in relation to Charles I's character and aims.

Answer 1

The extract states that Charles had an unsuitable personality for governing his kingdoms. Also, because of his stubborn personality, he was unable to work with Parliament. This shows that he was fundamentally unable to act as a successful monarch.

Answer 2

This extract acknowledges that Charles had faith in his own abilities. However, it argues that this self-confidence resulted in regular disputes with Parliament and different 'powerful interest groups'. The author argues that, as a result, Charles saw Parliament merely as a 'rubber stamp' and did not believe that it should have a central role in advising the monarch.

EXTRACT A

From C. Carlton, 'Three British Revolutions and the personality of Kingship' in J.A. Pocock (ed.) Three British Revolutions: 1641, 1688, 1776 (1980).

An authoritarian personality, Charles was incapable of conceding at a time when compromises were desperately demanded from the English monarchy. He was full of that outward self-certainty (manifest in such doctrines as divine right) that only intense inner doubt can engender... Charles saw his kingly role as a judge to whom issues were taken for decision... not that of a bargainer who settled disputes between rival branches of government, and negotiated settlements with other powerful interest groups. No wonder Charles' parliaments all ended in discord... Charles was psychologically incapable of dealing with a parliament that was anything more than a rubber stamp.

Financial weakness and reform under James I

Underlying problems

Elizabeth faced financial difficulties before her death in 1603. This meant that James struggled to raise adequate revenue due to a number of underlying issues from Elizabeth's reign:

- Elizabeth had inherited a Crown debt of over £250,000 upon becoming queen.
- Inflation had been affecting the value of commodities and money throughout the Tudor period.
- A series of bad harvests in the 1590s added to the rising price of crops.
- Elizabeth had been fighting intermittently with Spain since 1585. This meant that she could not rely on ordinary revenue and was forced to sell Crown assets.
- Elizabeth resorted to forced loans (that in reality she never intended to pay back) totalling £100,000 in the late 1590s in order to pay for the war with Spain. This created resentment from the Political Nation and a level of distrust surrounding the future levying of taxes.
- Elizabeth's shortfall in revenue stood at nearly £90,000 in 1600.

Finance: success

- Robert Cecil, Earl of Salisbury, became James's chief financial adviser. He introduced a Book of Rates in 1608, which outlined the amount of customs duties to be paid on various items. These included a number of new duties, known as impositions.
- Cecil died in 1612 and Lionel Cranfield became James's most high profile financial adviser after 1618. Cranfield established commissions to investigate royal finance and expenditure, and was able to reduce spending by half.
- Elizabeth had exploited the process whereby monopolies producing certain goods were sold to individuals or companies, and James continued this practice. James used monopolies as a way to reward his royal favourites, particularly George Villiers, Duke of Buckingham, after 1618.
- Between 1603 and 1613 the English economy was relatively buoyant and exports of the country's main export, cloth, increased steadily. This was to be interrupted by a recession from 1614.

Finance: failure

- The 1608 Book of Rates was resented because entirely new customs duties were introduced for some goods.
- In 1610, the Great Contract was introduced by Cecil. According to the Contract, James would agree to abandon his right to claim a number of feudal taxes including wardship and purveyance in return for an annual grant approved by Parliament. Both James and the House of Commons ultimately rejected the terms.
- James had a wife and children, and as a result faced financial pressures that the childless Elizabeth never had to consider.
- James mistakenly believed that England would provide him with significantly more wealth than Scotland and this led to accusations of financial irresponsibility. He gave at least £100,000 to his Scottish courtiers between 1606 and 1611.
- Despite Cranfield's financial reforms, the trust shown to him by James resulted in him profiting greatly from the power delegated to him. Cranfield controlled the system of patronage and took bribes in exchange for appointments and titles.
- In 1624, Parliament passed the Statute of Monopolies, greatly reducing the Crown's ability to sell monopolies and patents.
- Cloth exports decreased drastically from 1614, which led a merchant, William Cockayne, to devise a plan to complete all cloth production (including the final dyeing and finishing usually done by the Dutch) in England. This was intended to reduce Dutch influence over the process, and James granted Cockayne a monopoly over cloth exports. When the Dutch refused to purchase the finished cloth from the English, sales slumped and failed to recover.

! Eliminate irrelevance a

Below are an exam-style question and a paragraph written in answer to this question. Read the paragraph and identify parts of the paragraph that are not directly relevant to the question. Draw a line through the information that is irrelevant and justify your deletions in the margin.

How accurate is it to say that James's financial inheritance made relations between Crown and Parliament impossible to maintain between 1603 and 1629?

The financial situation that James inherited from Elizabeth made relations with Parliament very difficult. Elizabeth had been at war with Spain from 1585, which became very expensive. This rivalry with Spain culminated with the Spanish dispatching the Armada to attack England in 1588, only to be repelled by the English. Elizabeth relied on forced loans, which she never intended to pay back, and this created resentment from the gentry and other members of the political class. Despite this poor financial inheritance, the debt inherited by James was similar to that inherited by Elizabeth in 1558.

i Develop the detail a

Below is an essay title and a paragraph written in answer to this question. The paragraph contains a limited amount of detail. Annotate the paragraph to add additional detail to the answer.

How successful were James I's financial policies in the years 1603–1625?

Between 1603 and 1625 James made a number of attempts to reform the nation's finances. He introduced new excise duties, known as 'impositions', and this helped to an extent. In the early years of his reign the economy was in a relatively strong position, and cloth exports increased. However, the Great Contract failed, which meant that both James and Parliament continued to resent each other.

Financial weakness and reform under Charles I

Economic inheritance

There was an economic depression accompanied by poor harvests in the early 1620s. The royal debt stood at £900,000 in 1620, and when Parliament met in 1621 and 1624, MPs were reluctant to grant James subsidies. When Charles succeeded to the throne in 1625 he found the Treasury virtually empty as a result of his father's frivolous spending. James had inherited a Crown debt of £400,000, and as we have seen, thought nothing of spending tens of thousands of pounds on his wardrobe or pensions for his Scottish followers at the royal court.

The impact of foreign policy

Charles involved England in the Thirty Years' War on the Protestant side. His commander-in-chief was the Duke of Buckingham, who embarked on a number of foreign policy ventures, all of which ended in failure and financial ruin. The excessive influence of Buckingham over the king was one of the main grievances that ultimately led to the opposition attacking Charles in the 1628 Parliament.

1625

The inherited financial problems led to confrontation between Charles and Parliament when they first met.

- Charles asked for a loan of £60,000 from the City of London merchants.
- When the Commons met they refused to grant Charles an excise tax, Tonnage and Poundage, for life. It was customary for a new monarch to be granted this tax.
- MPs offered to grant Charles Tonnage and Poundage for only one year, which contributed to his decision to dissolve Parliament.

1626

Desperate for money to continue his foreign policy ventures, Charles called another Parliament and faced similar problems.

- Parliament refused to engage in debates over finance and instead attacked Buckingham, who was viewed with suspicion and had recently been involved in a number of foreign policy failures.
- Charles dissolved Parliament and issued a forced loan. Those who refused to pay were threatened with imprisonment or conscription into the army.

1627

- Over £200,000 was successfully raised from the forced loan.
- Despite the loan raising more money than Parliament had granted before, almost one-third of the expected money was not paid.
- A number of gentry who refused to pay the forced loan were imprisoned, and five of them issued writs of habeas corpus.
- The gentry involved in the so-called 'Five Knights Case' were told by the court that they had been detained by special command of the king, a decision that effectively approved royal tyranny.

1628

In further need of funds, Charles attempted to pass a Bill that would provide him with five subsidies. After delaying tactics from the Commons, the Bill was passed only after Charles promised to give his assent to the Petition of Right (see page 20).

Develop the detail

a

Below are a sample essay title and a paragraph written in answer to this question. The paragraph contains a limited amount of detail. Annotate the paragraph to add additional detail to the answer.

'The main threats to the stability of Charles's government in the years 1625 to 1629 were economic rather than religious.' How far do you agree with this opinion?

> Charles's difficult relations with Parliament demonstrate the fact that economic problems were at the heart of most major issues. From the beginning, Charles had disagreements with Parliament over financial issues. Parliament refused to grant him the right to collect Tonnage and Poundage. Charles resorted to a forced loan in order to collect adequate revenue and this caused resentment from the Political Nation.

 Introducing an argument

Below are a sample essay title, a list of key points to be made in the essay, and a simple introduction and conclusion. Read the question, the plan, and the introduction and conclusion. Rewrite the introduction and conclusion in order to develop an argument.

'The main threats to the stability of Charles I's government in the years 1625-29 arose from financial rather than political problems.' How far do you agree with this opinion?

Key points

- Economic inheritance
- Charles's relations with Parliament
- Charles's personality and behaviour
- Charles's advisers

Introduction

> In the years 1625 to 1629 Charles I's government faced a number of problems. The financial problems faced ultimately led to Charles dissolving Parliament in 1629.

Conclusion

> In conclusion, the main threats to Charles's government resulted from the economic situation. There would have been no major threat to Charles's government had it not been for the economic and financial situation in England.

Religious issues under James I

Religious views

As a strong believer in the Divine Right of Kings, James held the authority of the Church in high regard. He was fiercely loyal to Protestantism and although he had misgivings about the more extreme Presbyterian Reformation that had taken place in Scotland, he was suspicious of Catholicism. James wanted to achieve stability and unity of religion across all three of his kingdoms, and this meant attempting to find a middle way between the high-church tradition, which emphasised the authority of the clergy and rituals similar to those found in the Catholic Church, and the low-church tradition, which favoured simplicity in worship.

The Millenary Petition and the Puritans

The Millenary Petition was produced by a group of Puritans when James took the throne in 1603, and it contained the signatures of 1,000 ministers. Its authors made a number of important statements regarding the state of the Church:

- They stated that they respected James's position as Supreme Governor of the Church and were not interested in breaking up the Church of England.
- Despite the Protestant Reformation, the Church of England had not left behind many Catholic practices.
- Church services were too difficult for ordinary people to understand and decorations in churches distracted the congregation from the true purpose of religion.

As a king keen to be viewed as someone who promoted ideological debate, James arranged the Hampton Court conference in response to the Petition. Representatives from both sides of the religious spectrum were invited.

The Hampton Court Conference, 1604

Outcome of the conference

The Anglican bishops who attended the conference were reluctant to give way to the demands of the Puritans. James met the bishops and some changes were agreed in response to the Millenary Petition, including the weakening of the authority of the church courts.

Suggestions from the Puritans that the church should be reformed along Presbyterian lines (without a hierarchy of bishops) were rejected by James. He did, however, accept their suggestion that a new translation of the Bible should be made and the new version, known as the King James Bible, was completed in 1611.

The bishops were generally satisfied with the outcome of the conference. However, the more radical Puritans were not. Conformity to the Church as inherited by James in 1603 was to be enforced.

Aftermath

Dissatisfaction from the Puritans continued after the conference and in 1610 the Commons presented James with a Petition of Religion. It criticised James's attacks on non-conformists and the removal of Puritan ministers. James did little to reassure the Puritans and in 1622 he issued an edict attacking travelling Puritan preachers and urging them to conform.

Catholicism

James was the intended victim of a number of pro-Catholic conspiracies, the most famous of which was the Gunpowder Plot of 1605. Despite the alarm this caused James, he was surprisingly lenient towards Catholics, and a moderate Oath of Allegiance was issued in 1606, requiring Catholics to deny the pope's pre-eminence.

The Scottish Kirk

James desired unity in the Church and his Scottish policy was no exception. He wanted to unite the English and Scottish Churches, and in 1618 he issued the Five Articles of Perth, which stated that Holy Communion should be taken kneeling, religious holidays celebrated and confirmation performed by bishops. The Articles were reluctantly passed by the Scottish Parliament and no further reform was tabled.

Mind map

Use the information on the opposite page to add detail to the mind map below.

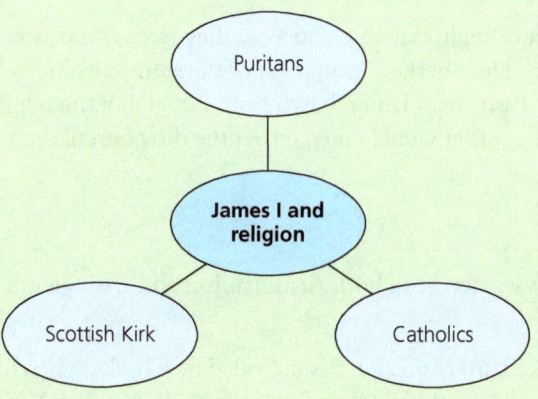

Puritans

James I and religion

Scottish Kirk

Catholics

 Use own knowledge to support or contradict

Below is an extract to read. You are asked to summarise the interpretation about James's reputation and then develop a counter-argument.

Interpretation offered by the source:

_____

_____

Counter-argument:

_____

_____

_____

_____

EXTRACT A

From A. Stilma, A King Translated: The Writings of King James VI & I and their Interpretation in the Low Countries, 1593-1603 *(2012)*.

Scholarly opinion on how James fulfilled his role as King has shifted substantially in recent years. James's reputation has long been coloured by the hostile accounts of his reign that appeared later in the seventeenth century... but historians have largely moved beyond the image of James as a bumbling autocrat, the 'wisest fool in Christendom' who cared little for public opinion because he valued no-one's opinion but his own. If anything, given how suspicious our own society is of power and the powerful, the recent appreciation of James's shrewdness and subtlety seems to go hand in hand with an increasing tendency to portray him (in equally overstated terms) as a ruthless Machiavellian manipulator.

Religious issues under Charles I

Charles's religious views

Charles was naturally drawn towards high-church practices as they were compatible with his preference for order and ceremony. He inherited a suspicion of Puritanism from his father and with so many of his opponents in Parliament being drawn from this end of the religious spectrum, it was only natural that conflict would emerge over the direction of the Church of England.

Promotion of Arminianism

Charles demonstrated his close association with both Arminianism and Catholicism in a number of ways in the years 1625–29.

- In 1625, the Arminian cleric Richard Montagu was defended by Charles when he argued that Calvinist beliefs were incompatible with the Church in a pamphlet entitled A *New Gag for an Old Goose*.
- Montagu was appointed Charles's personal chaplain.
- In 1628, Montagu was appointed Bishop of Chichester at the death of the former Bishop, George Carleton, who was known for possessing anti-Arminian views.
- Another high-profile royal chaplain was Roger Maynwaring, appointed in 1626. He was a firm supporter of royal absolutism and claimed that Charles's right to collect the forced loan was given to him by God and that Parliament did not need to be consulted over taxation.
- In 1626, Charles issued a proclamation that forbade the public discussion of sensitive religious topics. This was aimed at silencing his Puritan critics.
- The Archbishop of Canterbury, George Abbot, was suspended in 1627 for refusing to grant an Arminian sermon and his allies were sidelined.
- Other Arminians, such as John Howson, Bishop of Oxford, were supported by Charles. Howson had previously come into conflict with Abbott over the concept of predestination.
- William Laud, the most influential of the Arminians, was appointed to the Privy Council in 1628 when he became Bishop of London.

The York House Conference

A religious conference was held at the Duke of Buckingham's home at York House in February 1626. Arminians were pitted against the Puritan opposition and the conference only served to harden Charles's religious views.

- Both clergy and laymen were represented at the conference.
- The primary aim of the conference was to resolve the ongoing dispute between Puritans and Arminians.
- A second aim was to defend Richard Montagu from prosecution by the House of Commons.
- The influential Buckingham made it clear that he sided firmly with the Arminians, and by implication this meant that the Arminian arguments had royal backing.
- Charles himself showed his contempt for the Puritan opposition by refusing to attend the conference.
- Puritan MPs were infuriated by Buckingham's promotion of the Arminians.

Spot the mistake **a**

Below are a sample exam question and a paragraph written in answer to this question. Why does this paragraph not get high praise? What is wrong with the focus of the answer in this paragraph?

To what extent was the breakdown in relations between Crown and Parliament by 1629 caused by religious issues?

Religious conflict was widespread under both James I and Charles I. Charles promoted Arminian chaplains and bishops at the expense of bishops such as Abbott, who was suspended in 1627 for refusing to grant an Arminian sermon. Many of Charles's opponents in Parliament were Puritans, and in 1626 a conference was held at York House to resolve differences in opinion.

 Simple essay style

Below is a sample AS exam question. Use your own knowledge and the information on the opposite page to produce a plan for this question. Choose four general points, and provide three pieces of specific information to support each general point. Once you have planned your essay, write the introduction and conclusion for the essay. The introduction should list the points to be discussed in the essay. The conclusion should summarise the key points and justify which point was the most important.

'Religious conflict was more important than financial issues in causing conflict between Crown and Parliament between 1603 and 1629.' Explain why you agree or disagree with this view.

James I and Parliament

First Parliament, 1604–10

First session: March–July 1604

As James was now king of both England and Scotland, he explored the possibility of a closer legal union between the two kingdoms. Proposals for this union were drafted by Robert Cecil and immediately faced opposition from Parliament in its first session. This overshadowed any prospect of reasonable dialogue.

Second session: November 1605–May 1606

Meeting in the wake of the Gunpowder Plot, MPs showed significantly more unity and legislation was passed targeting Catholics, although a financial settlement was harder to come by. Eventually, James was granted subsidies worth almost £400,000.

1607–10

Parliament did not meet at all between July 1607 and February 1610. Cecil's introduction of The Great Contract became the main focus of the 1610 session but it was eventually shelved by both James and the Commons.

1614: The 'Addled Parliament'

The issue of impositions was raised as soon as the 1614 Parliament met and the Commons sent a message to the Lords asking for a conference, with a view to petitioning the king against further impositions. The Lords refused to debate the issue and the Bishop of Lincoln, Richard Neile, made a speech announcing that impositions were a matter of royal prerogative. James soon realised that this Parliament would not grant him the subsidies he needed and it was dissolved after just two months.

1621 Parliament

The Thirty Years' War had begun in 1618 and therefore foreign policy became a key issue in the 1621 Parliament. James had ruled alone for seven years and this lack of parliamentary consultation caused resentment from a number of MPs. In need of money to assist his son-in-law, Fredrick V of Bohemia, in the war, James reluctantly agreed to the impeachment of his Lord Chancellor, Francis Bacon, for corruption. James announced his intention to marry his son, Charles, to a Spanish princess and dissolved the Parliament when this was met with vocal opposition in February 1622.

1624 Parliament

James broke off the Spanish Match when Spain demanded that the eldest son of Frederick V and James's daughter, Elizabeth, marry a daughter of the Catholic Holy Roman Emperor. James was now resolved on war with Spain and needed funds, so called Parliament for the last time in 1624. The Commons focused on attacking Cranfield, who they viewed as being corrupt and self-serving. Relations between king and the Parliament were relatively positive, with James being granted a number of subsidies to fund a war, and the session only ended when James died in March 1625.

Conclusion: Charles's parliamentary inheritance

There were a number of problems that were never fully settled in the years 1603–25 and would continue to cause problems for Charles I.

- The issue of royal finances caused considerable friction and the only prospect of a realistic settlement (The Great Contract) was abandoned.
- James's choice of advisers resulted in a number of impeachments and resistance from Parliament. When James died, Buckingham smoothly moved in as Charles's favourite.
- Religious divisions were evident throughout these years and James was always suspicious of the Puritan faction, as Charles would be in later years.

Quick quizzes at **www.hoddereducation.co.uk/myrevisionnotes**

RAG – Rate the timeline

Below is a sample exam-style question and a timeline. Read the question, study the timeline and using three coloured pens, put a red, amber or green star next to the events to show:

Red: events and policies that have no relevance to the question

Amber: events and policies that have some significance to the question

Green: events and policies that are directly relevant to the question

How far do you agree that the divisions between James and Parliament in the years 1603–25 were caused by financial issues?

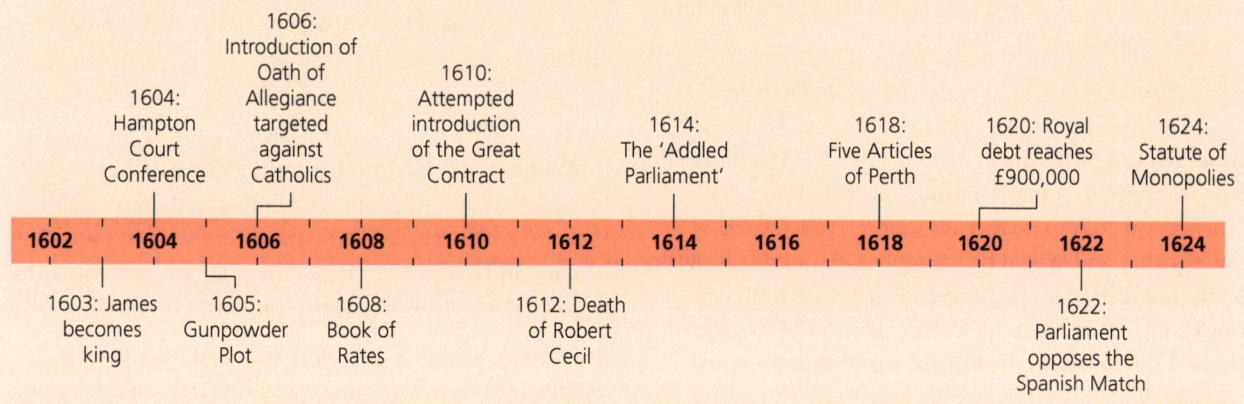

How far do you agree?

Read the extract below. Using the table, summarise each of its arguments. Use your knowledge to agree or contradict.

Arguments in extract	Knowledge that corroborates	Knowledge that contradicts
1		
2		
3		

EXTRACT A

From M. Ashley, England in the Seventeenth Century *(1973).*

King James sometimes made foolish or irritating remarks in his speeches to Parliament, but he can scarcely be blamed for believing that he governed by 'divine right' or that he inherited 'prerogative powers' that could not be questioned. In the seventeenth century every authority claimed that it ruled by divine right... King James I and his advisers had the good sense not to press too hard or too far. In the struggle that lay ahead it was Parliament, not the King, that threw out the challenge and demanded that the sovereign should submit to a modification of his traditional rights. Thus since the King was incapable of living within his income out of the royal revenues, he was always on the defensive against a growing opposition.

Charles I and the state of relations between Crown and Parliament by 1629

Early relations

As discussed on page 16, the 1625 and 1626 Parliaments were dominated by:

- attacks on Buckingham
- debates over the funding of wars
- disputes about Charles's right to collect certain taxes (such as Tonnage and Poundage).

After dissolving the 1626 Parliament, Charles issued the forced loan and faced opposition in the Five Knights Case. Buckingham's inept diplomacy led to war and a failed attempt to support a Protestant rebellion in La Rochelle in 1627. The recruits sent to France were of poor quality and lacked basic supplies. Around half of the 6,000 English soldiers sent to La Rochelle died when Buckingham besieged the town, and most of England blamed Buckingham directly for the disaster.

Charles hoped to fund a continuation of the war and recalled Parliament in 1628. As an act of good faith, he released some of those imprisoned for refusing to pay the forced loan.

The 1628 Parliament

Parliament had tried to impeach Buckingham in the past, and Charles knew this was a possibility when he assembled Parliament again in 1628. He demanded that he would only work with Parliament if they did not attack Buckingham. Charles wanted to send another force to La Rochelle, despite the previous failures, and MPs, led by Sir John Eliot, insisted that their grievances be heard before taxes were granted.

The Petition of Right

Eliot and his allies, including Sir Edward Coke, John Selden and Sir Thomas Wentworth (later Earl of Strafford), prepared a carefully worded document, the Petition of Right, and presented it to Charles. Its clauses included the following:

- There should be no imprisonment without trial and the decision made in the Five Knights Case should be reversed.
- There should be no taxation without parliamentary consent.
- Citizens should not be asked to pay forced loans.
- The forced billeting of soldiers should not be allowed.
- There should be no martial law.

The authors claimed that these rights had been enshrined in law centuries earlier, but Charles disagreed and initially refused to agree to the demands. Eventually, in June 1628, he agreed to the Petition, believing that he would be able to continue ruling as he had done previously without repercussions. Parliament consented to the taxes asked for by Charles but also began to attack Buckingham once again. Charles promptly closed the parliamentary session.

The state of relations in 1629

In August 1628, Buckingham was assassinated in Portsmouth by a disgruntled sailor named John Felton. When Charles recalled Parliament for its second session in January 1629, its leaders hoped to make progress now that the influence of Buckingham had been removed.

Parliament, again led by Eliot, criticised both Charles's methods of collecting money and his Arminian religion. In March 1629, Eliot issued the Three Resolutions, which included the following:

- A denouncement of Charles's Arminian advisers.
- A statement announcing that the levying of Tonnage and Poundage was unacceptable.
- Those who paid Tonnage and Poundage were labelled as enemies of the Kingdom.

Charles had ordered Parliament to be adjourned before the Resolutions had been read, and the Speaker of the Commons refused to delay it. A group of MPs led by Denzil Holles and Sir John Eliot held the Speaker in his chair until the Resolutions had been passed, amid much shouting and confusion.

A Royal proclamation was then drawn up whereby Charles announced the formal dissolution of Parliament in March 1629. Eliot and eight of his allies were arrested and imprisoned. Parliament would not meet again for another 11 years.

! Eliminate irrelevance

Below are a sample essay title and a paragraph written in answer to this question. Read the paragraph and identify parts of the paragraph that are not directly relevant to the question. Draw a line through the information that is irrelevant and justify your deletions in the margin.

> To what extent was discontent over the role of Buckingham the main reason for conflicts between Crown and Parliament in the years 1614–1629?

Buckingham's role is crucially important in understanding Charles's poor relationship with Parliament in these years. Buckingham had been the favourite of Charles's father, James I, and held great sway over both men. It was highly likely that Parliament would attempt to impeach Buckingham in 1628, and Charles took measures to avoid this. It could be argued that the Petition of Right was written as a direct result of Buckingham's actions, as it made a number of references to the billeting of soldiers and the use of martial law.

i Turning assertion into argument

Below are a series of definitions, a sample exam question and two sample conclusions. One of the conclusions achieves a high mark because it contains an argument. The other achieves a lower mark because it contains only description and assertion. Identify which is which. The mark scheme on page 5 will help you.

- **Description:** a detailed account.
- **Assertion:** a statement of fact or an opinion which is not supported by a reason.
- **Reason:** a statement which explains or justifies something.
- **Argument:** an assertion justified with a reason.

> To what extent were the desires of the early Stuarts to become involved in wars the most important reason for the breakdown of Crown and Parliament relations by 1629?

Answer 1

Overall, there is clearly some evidence that the desires of James and Charles to become involved in wars were an important reason for poor parliamentary relations. First, James wanted to become involved in the Thirty Years' War from 1618 and recalled Parliament after seven years in order to ask for subsidies. He later wanted to start a war with Spain and Parliament demanded the impeachment of Cranfield as a condition of providing funds. Charles attempted to relieve besieged Protestants at La Rochelle and this angered Parliament further against Buckingham. However, there were other reasons for poor relations, such as religious differences, highlighted at the Hampton Court Conference of 1604, and the belief that both kings had in Divine Right monarchy.

Answer 2

In conclusion, by embarking on foreign wars both Charles and James caused relations with Parliament to become extremely strained. However, the wars only exacerbated existing problems and brought them to the surface. James inherited debt from Elizabeth and Charles inherited £400,000 of debt from James. This meant that MPs were never likely to approve extravagant spending, and they were well aware that funding a war was probably the biggest outlay a country could make. Both Charles and James believed strongly in Divine Right, and this meant that they saw calling Parliament as an occasional necessity. Therefore they were unable to comprehend why Parliament opposed them and their advisers when they were called in order to fund wars. In this sense, the wars highlighted an already tense situation.

Exam focus (AS-level)

Below is a sample high-level answer to an AS-level-style question. Read it and the comments around it.

'Involvement in foreign wars resulted in the breakdown of relations between Crown and Parliament in the years 1603 to 1629.' Explain why you agree or disagree with this view.

Both James's and Charles's governments faced a number of serious challenges from Parliament in the years 1603–29, and there is no doubt that their attempts to become involved in the Thirty Years' War caused many of them. If it was not for their foreign policy ambitions, the opposition in Parliament would not have been as vocal and aggressive. If this foreign policy had succeeded, major financial problems would not have been as serious. As well as these issues, a belief from both monarchs in Divine Right and their controversial attempts at financial reform caused serious difficulties.

James wanted to become involved in the Thirty Years' War to assist his son-in-law, Frederick V. A clear link can be made here to a lack of financial success, as Parliament insisted on the impeachment of the Lord Chancellor, Francis Bacon, in exchange for giving James subsidies. The English had little recent experience of warfare, particularly on land, and English involvement in the war arguably exacerbated conflicts that already existed. For example, Buckingham was viewed with suspicion and when Charles's first Parliament met in 1625 a number of members wanted to impeach him. Buckingham was chosen as Commander-in-Chief for the failed expedition to assist French Protestants at La Rochelle. A number of clauses in the Petition of Right of 1628 concerned martial law and the forced billeting of soldiers, which were direct responses to Charles's failed foreign policy. Overall, James's and Charles's involvement in war angered an already dissatisfied Parliament and gave MPs further excuses to attempt to erode the royal prerogative.

Financial issues were also central to the conflicts between Crown and Parliament in these years. James attempted to introduce a Book of Rates in 1608 and the Great Contract of 1610 was abandoned by Parliament. However, it can be argued that James's inherent misunderstanding of the English political system (he assumed England was much wealthier than his former kingdom of Scotland) meant that he was always destined to fail. There were some successes for James in his attempts at financial reform, such as Cranfield's commissions into royal expenditure, which reduced spending by half. When Charles first met with Parliament in 1625, he asked for a loan of £60,000 from the City of London merchants, which created resentment. Already suspicious of Charles because of his religious and foreign policy, the Commons refused to grant him the right to collect Tonnage and Poundage for life, and instead only offered it for one year. Charles dissolved Parliament and issued a forced loan to the gentry. Problems were made worse when a number of gentry who refused to pay the loan were imprisoned. Five of them issued writs of habeas corpus and were told that they had been detained by special command of the king. Dissatisfaction with the result of the 'Five Knights Case' contributed to the demands found in the Petition of Right. As well as the clauses regarding war, the authors stated that there should be no taxation without Parliamentary consent and that citizens should not be asked to pay forced loans. It is clear therefore that financial issues were central to problems, but a number of them developed as a result of foreign policy decisions and his economic inheritance.

This is an introduction that is focused on the question. The candidate demonstrates awareness of the major issues and it gives some indication of where the essay intends to go.

This paragraph shows detailed knowledge of the foreign policy ventures James and Charles embarked on and the impact this had on relations with their Parliaments.

Having dealt with the issue of war, this paragraph deals with financial issues. Note the last few sentences which draw a comparison between two of the factors discussed in the essay.

Both James and Charles believed strongly in Divine Right and religious division in general was central to their inability to govern effectively in these years. Even before he became King of England, James wrote that monarchs should be able to wield unrestrained power. James therefore saw Parliament as an occasional necessity and ruled without it for years at a time. Charles showed that he clearly wanted to associate himself with both Arminianism and Catholicism through his religious policy. As early as 1625, he defended Richard Montagu, who had attacked Calvinism, and Montagu was made Charles's personal chaplain. Charles also suspended Archbishop Abbott in 1627 for refusing to grant an Arminian sermon, and William Laud was elevated at Abbott's expense. As well as his clear preference for Arminians within the Church of England, Charles had made it clear for a number of years that he wanted a Catholic wife. Coupled with Charles's firm belief in Divine Right and his obsession with ceremonies, order and ritual, his religious beliefs served to promote suspicion amongst the political nation. Many of the MPs who opposed him in the House of Commons, such as John Eliot, were Puritans and were already suspicious of James I. Charles had attempted to promote the Protestant cause in Europe in the Thirty Years' War, but his domestic policy clearly showed that he was happy for religious conflict to continue.

In conclusion, it is clear that both James and Charles faced a number of challenges in these years. Some of these already existed before they became King and others were potentially avoidable. Their desire to assist the Protestant cause in the Thirty Years' War seemed to conflict with their domestic religious policy, and this created suspicion amongst Puritans. Foreign policy ventures also made existing financial issues worse, and it could therefore be argued that involvement in war was the most important catalyst in causing tensions. Their reputations as military leaders were tarnished and a deep mistrust of their advisers, especially Buckingham, arose from foreign policy failures.

This paragraph moves on to Divine Right and religious issues and provides a good amount of evidence to support this, although it is balanced more towards Charles than James.

The conclusion pulls together the argument that was initiated and developed throughout the essay. The essay thus presents a consistent argument.

This is a sustained response that would obtain Level 5. The candidate explores the factor given in the question but also examines related factors. The answer is thorough and detailed, clearly engages with the question and offers a balanced and carefully reasoned argument which is sustained throughout the essay.

Reverse engineering

The best essays are based on careful plans. Read the essay and the comments and try to work out the general points of the plan used to write the essay. Once you have done this, jot down the specific examples used to support each general point.

Exam focus (A-level)

Below is a sample high level answer to an A-level style question. Read it and the comments around it.

'The religious beliefs of the early Stuart kings caused the religious and political disputes that existed in the years 1603–29.' Assess the validity of this view.

There is debate about how far James's and Charles's religious beliefs were responsible for the religious and political issues facing England in the years 1603–29. It can be argued that their belief in Divine Right, James's reluctance to listen to the views of the Puritans and Charles's decision to elevate Arminian clergy meant that disputes were inevitable. There are, however, a number of other factors that may explain these issues, such as wider conflicts with Parliament – which had both political and religious grievances – and financial issues that hampered the progress of both kings. On balance, it is clear that if both kings had taken a fair approach to negotiations with the Political Nation and religious minorities from the beginning, tensions would have been much lower.

> The introduction quickly gets to grips with the question. It provides good hints of where its argument intends to go – that is, James and Charles (and their religious policies) were ultimately responsible for the escalation of tensions in these years.

James held a strong belief in Divine Right and publicly stated that he believed God placed kings on the throne and that monarchs should be able to wield unrestrained power. As a result of this he had little need for Parliament and saw it as an occasional advisory body. Charles also believed in Divine Right and was keen to promote Arminians within the Church and his Arminian advisers, such as William Laud, were held in high regard.

James organised the Hampton Court conference in response to the Puritan Millenary Petition in 1604. Here, James rejected reforming the Church along Presbyterian lines although he did show a degree of sympathy by issuing a new version of the Bible. He urged Puritan preachers to conform in 1622 and made it clear in the Five Articles of Perth that the Scottish Kirk should be reformed along Anglican lines. James's reluctance to give concessions to the Puritans only stored up problems for Charles, who came into conflict with them after 1625. He promoted Arminians such as Montagu at the expense of George Abbott, who was suspended for refusing to grant an Arminian sermon. Charles also refused to attend the York House Conference, and made it clear that he sided with the Arminians. There was a clear understanding among members of the Political Nation that the religion of the Stuart Kings was associated with their more absolutist policies and it is no coincidence that many of the MPs who opposed them were Puritan in their religious sympathies.

> These paragraphs deal with the given factor of religious preferences. They show precise knowledge and relate it well to the problems faced.

A belief in Divine Right gave James and Charles the impression their rule should be unquestioned, and this led to financial decisions that were not popular. James attempted to introduce a Book of Rates in 1608, and the Great Contract of 1610 was abandoned by Parliament. However, it can be argued that James's inherent misunderstanding of the English political system (he assumed England was much wealthier than his former kingdom of Scotland) meant that he was always destined to fail. There were some successes for James in his attempts at financial reform, such as Cranfield's commissions into royal expenditure, which reduced spending by half. When Charles first met with Parliament in 1625, he asked for a loan of £60,000 from the City of London merchants, which created resentment. Already suspicious of Charles because of his religious and foreign policy, the Commons refused to grant him the right to collect Tonnage and Poundage for life, and instead only offered it for one year. Charles dissolved Parliament and issued a forced loan to the gentry. Problems were made worse when a number of gentry who refused to pay the loan were imprisoned. Five

> Again the candidate shows excellent knowledge. The second paragraph introduces a counter-argument suggesting that the economic inheritance could be to blame.

of them issued writs of habeas corpus and were told that they had been detained by special command of the King. Dissatisfaction with the result of the 'Five Knights Case' contributed to the demands found in the Petition of Right.

It could be argued, however, that the financial inheritance of the Stuart kings meant that they were destined to fail. Inflation had been affecting the value of commodities throughout the Tudor period and Elizabeth had been attempting to fight an expensive war with Spain. She had already resorted to forced loans totalling £100,000 and she passed the debt on to James.

Wider conflicts with Parliament were also to blame for both political and religious issues in these years. James's first Parliament in 1604 came to blows with the monarchy because of a suggestion that there should be a closer union with Scotland, although in the wake of the Gunpowder Plot of 1605 it granted £400,000 of subsidies and relations were more cordial. James ruled without Parliament between 1614 and 1621 and this led to resentment from MPs, who insisted on the impeachment of his Lord Chancellor, Francis Bacon.

The political opposition Charles faced in Parliament was led by a number of fierce critics, such as John Eliot, who pushed for as many concessions as possible. In 1628 Parliament issued the Petition of Right and in 1629 Eliot issued the Three Resolutions, which included an attack of Charles's Arminian advisers and a statement announcing that Tonnage and Poundage should be illegal. There is a strong case to suggest that Eliot's demands here were unreasonable, because it had become customary for monarchs to collect Tonnage and Poundage with the consent of Parliament. Charles had ordered Parliament to be adjourned before the Resolutions had been read, and the Speaker of the Commons refused to delay it. A group of MPs led by Eliot and Denzil Holles held the Speaker in his chair until the Resolutions passed. Despite these actions by the opposition, they were ultimately prompted by the actions of Charles, as criticisms of his religion, as well as his financial policies, were central to many of the attacks on his government.

In conclusion, it is clear that many of the political and religious issues in this period, although not all begun by James and Charles, were made worse as a result of their beliefs. In pursuing an Arminian religious policy and a financial policy that did not take into account the views of the political nation, James and Charles were destined to face opposition.

This paragraph begins to pull everything together – ahead of the conclusion. It links back to the introduction as it once again suggests that James and Charles were ultimately to blame for the problems of these years.

The conclusion is sharp and emphasises the main line of argument introduced earlier, although it is brief and does not weigh up the relative importance of the different factors presented.

This answer is a clear Level 5. It is both thorough and detailed. It clearly engages with the question and offers a balanced and carefully reasoned argument, which is sustained throughout the course of the essay.

What makes a good answer?

You have now considered two high-level essays. Use these two essays to make a bullet-pointed list of the characteristics of a top-level essay. Use this list when planning and writing your own practice exam essays.

2 Revolution, 1629–49

Divisions over religion during personal rule, 1629–40

Charles allowed Archbishop Laud a high degree of autonomy over Church affairs. Both men shared the same vision of a Church of England steeped in order and decorum. They were keen to promote Arminianism (see page 16).

The Beauty of Holiness

Charles and Laud demanded strict adherence to rules and the substitution of ritual and formality in place of the Puritan emphasis on individual prayer and preaching. Laud believed that a visit to church should be a stimulating experience for all the senses. This was reflected in his changes to the fabric and ordering of churches:

- Organs were installed and the singing of hymns was encouraged.
- Fonts were decorated.
- Statues and colour returned to churches.
- Stained glass was installed.
- The communion table was moved from the centre of the congregation to the east end of the church, where the Roman Catholic altar had always stood. It was also railed off from the congregation. This was a particularly objectionable change in the eyes of the Puritans.

The status of the clergy

As part of his quest for uniformity, Laud aimed to enhance the power of the Church hierarchy. He did this in a number of ways:

- He ordered bishops to visit each of their parishes at least once every three years.
- Archbishops were expected to report directly to Charles.
- A campaign against unlicensed preaching was launched.
- Priests were given jobs as Justices of the Peace (JPs) and a number of bishops sat on the Privy Council.
- The prerogative courts, especially the Star Chamber, were used to judge religious cases. Harsh punishments were inflicted on those who criticised Laud's reforms.

The Book of Sports

In 1618, James I had published a Book of Sports, and this was reissued by Charles in 1633. The Book permitted people to take part in a number of approved activities on Sundays, in reaction to the established Puritan belief that only worship and spiritual reflection should take place on Sundays.

The Feoffees of Impropriations

The increasingly popular practice of Puritan gentry buying up the right to appoint a local minister or right to collect the tithes that formed his salary (known as impropriated tithes) was strictly forbidden by Laud. A group known as the Feoffees, who had organised this practice in order to appoint their favoured Puritan clergy, was forced to disband.

Opposition to religious reforms

As part of his quest for uniformity in the church, Laud dismissed Puritan ministers and banned Puritan members of the gentry from appointing their own chaplains. Hundreds of clergy and as many as 20,000 Puritans emigrated to the North American colonies in the 1630s to escape persecution in England. As well as this opposition, congregations resented the economic cost of Laud's reforms. The restoration of organs and the beautifying of churches was an expensive undertaking.

Bastwick, Burton and Prynne

Three high profile Puritans who resisted Laud's reforms were all presented for trial in the Star Chamber in 1637 after previous individual cases against them had been pursued in the Church courts.

- John Bastwick was a doctor who wrote a number of tracts attacking bishops. The Star Chamber had banned the production of news sheets in 1632, and Laud took a personal interest in punishing those who continued to publish religious propaganda.
- Henry Burton was a minister whose sermons consistently deviated from those approved by Laud.
- William Prynne was a lawyer who wrote *Histriomastix*, a 1,000-page attack on the theatre and actresses, in 1632.
- All three men were fined £5,000, imprisoned for life and ordered to have part of their ears cut off.

Mind map

Use the information on the opposite page to add detail to the mind map below.

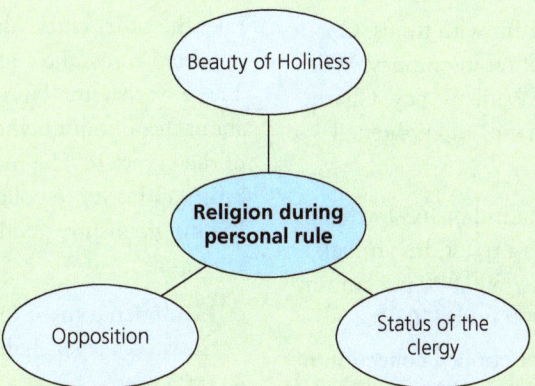

Comparing interpretations

With reference to the two extracts and your understanding of the historical context, which do you find more convincing in relation to the religious reforms of Charles I?

Compare the arguments in the two extracts, and use your contextual knowledge to decide which is more convincing.

You could shade the sections of each extract that you agree with.

Then set out the plan of the answer identifying agreements between the two extracts, and then disagreements, using your contextual knowledge.

Extract A argument(s)	Extract B argument(s)	Your contextual knowledge

EXTRACT A

From D. Smith, Constitutional Royalism and the Search for Settlement, *c1640–1649 (2010).*

1625 marked a critical turning-point in the ecclesiastical as well as the parliamentary and legal history of England... The Laudians extended existing arguments for conformity to enforce their own view of the rites and ceremonies of the Church. The insistence that the altar be moved to the east wall of the church and railed in; the concern for 'order' and decency'; the obsessive pursuit of the 'beauty of holiness'... To argue that Laud perceived himself less as an innovator than as a 'traditionalist' enforcing neglected aspects of the Elizabethan Church settlement is probably true, but cannot explain why so many contemporaries sense a definite change of direction from the late 1620s. It was not how Laud saw himself, but how others saw him, which proved so destabilising.

EXTRACT B

From L. James, William Laud, Charles I and the making of Scottish ecclesiastical policy, 1634–6 *in* Historical Research *(2017).*

The scope of Laud's personal contribution to the formulation and enforcement of the religious reforms which led to the collapse of royal government in three kingdoms has been a subject of interest for commentators and scholars, both past and present... It is natural that the king wished to appear as the author and instigator of policy, in order to procure obedience, and it suited Laud to have the mandate of royal approval upon which to act, particularly because he realized how controversial many of the measures were that he sought to implement... While he was adroit [skilful] at presenting himself as 'no master' in the process of policy formation, he can hardly be described as a mere servant either. His unique access to the monarch and their shared vision enabled him to act with a considerable degree of latitude in finalizing policies, provided that the monarch was seen as the dominant authority on which responsibility for a particular policy rested.

Personal rule and opposition, 1629–40

Methods of increasing revenue

Without a Parliament to provide him with funds, Charles had to embark on new methods of raising money. With the help of his Attorney General, William Noy, Charles set about reviving long forgotten taxes and tightened government spending.

- Charles signed the Treaty of Madrid in 1630, which ended hostilities with Spain. As a result, his annual spending on war reduced from £500,000 per annum in the 1620s to less than £70,000 in the 1630s.
- He raised £358,000 from the continued collection of Tonnage and Poundage.
- Fines for building on or encroaching on royal forests raised around £40,000. Monarchs had been able to levy these fines for centuries but many had not bothered to impose them.
- In 1630, Charles revived a medieval custom based on an Act from 1278, known as distraint of knighthood, whereby all those with land worth more than £40 per annum were expected to be knighted by the monarch on their coronation. If they had failed to present themselves at Charles's coronation, they were fined. Nearly £175,000 was raised as a result.
- Charles issued monopolies in return for a fee. A monopoly on the production of soap was given to a group of Catholic courtiers.
- Another feudal device that was collected more carefully was wardship revenue, which raised £55,000 per annum.
- The most infamous of Charles's taxes was Ship Money, a charge traditionally levied on coastal counties to pay for the navy. Most monarchs levied Ship Money once or twice during their reign, but Charles introduced it as an annual tax and charged all counties, not just those near the coast. It raised around £200,000 per annum between 1634 and 1640.

Opposition to financial reforms

Early opposition

- In 1629, a merchant, Richard Chambers, refused to pay Tonnage and Poundage after arguing that it affected those involved in trade disproportionately. He was imprisoned and fined £2,000.
- In 1634, Sir David Foulis, a Yorkshire gentleman, attempted an uprising against distraint of knighthood. It gained little support and may have been motivated more by Foulis's rivalry with Thomas Wentworth than any desire to attack the policies of the Crown.

John Hampden and Ship Money

Like the other taxes, Ship Money was generally paid as expected across the counties between 1634 and 1639. There were a small number of complaints, particularly about the amount being levied rather than the principle of the tax itself. The most high-profile challenge to the king's authority to collect Ship Money came from the Buckinghamshire gentleman and Puritan John Hampden.

- Hampden refused to pay Ship Money in 1636 and initiated a legal challenge against it.
- His lawyer in the case was Oliver St John. Both men were part of a circle of Puritan gentry and nobility who had been active in the Providence Island Company, a private shipping company.
- Charles decided to use Hampden's challenge as a test case in 1637.
- Seven judges ruled in favour of Charles's continued collection of the tax and five ruled against.
- According to contemporaries, the reaction of the gentry to the result of the case was generally hostile and created issues for Charles by the end of the decade.

As well as Hampden, others who showed dissatisfaction with Ship Money included Lord Saye and Sele, the Earl of Bedford and the Earl of Warwick. All of these men were part of the same Puritan network, and historians have argued that they would have resisted Charles's government regardless of his financial policies.

The taxpayers' strike, 1639

Most counties generally paid Ship Money in full, and in 1635-36 just under 98% of expected revenue was collected. In 1639, many of those expected to pay the tax refused and only 20% of expected revenue was collected. This was one of the key reasons why Charles recalled Parliament in 1640.

Charles embarked on the First Bishops' War with Scotland in 1639 (see page 30). Many taxpayers in England sympathised with the Scots as fellow Protestants and did not want to fund the war.

Simple essay style

Below is a sample exam question. Use your own knowledge and the information on the opposite page to produce a plan for this question. Choose four general points, and provide three pieces of specific information to support each general point. Once you have planned your essay, write the introduction and conclusion for the essay. The introduction should list the points to be discussed in the essay. The conclusion should summarise the key points and justify which point was the most important.

To what extent is it accurate to describe Charles's religious reforms as his greatest failure in the years 1629–1640?

 ## Spectrum of importance

Below are a sample essay-style question and a list of general points which could be used to answer the question. Use your own knowledge and the information in this section to reach a judgement about the importance of these general points to the question posed. Write numbers on the spectrum below to indicate their relative importance. Having done this, write a brief justification of your placement, explaining why some of these factors are more important than others. The resulting diagram could form the basis of an essay plan.

How accurate is it to describe the period from 1629–1640 as 11 years of tyranny?

1 The role of Charles I

2 The role of Laud and Church reforms

3 Financial reforms

4 Actions of the opposition

5 The influence of Catholicism at court

Least important ←——————————————————————→ Most important

Scotland and Ireland, 1629–40

Scotland

Charles left Scotland when he was just four years old and only returned for his Scottish coronation in 1633. He was out of touch with Scottish affairs and surrounded himself with anglicised Scots who falsely believed they had a sound grasp of Scottish opinion. Opposition in Scotland took the following form:

- Charles had already created resentment in 1625 when he passed the Revocation Act, effectively nullifying the claims of Scottish nobles to disputed lands. Under the Act, all church and royal land lost since 1540 was taken back for the Crown.

- The Protestant Reformation in Scotland had gone further than it had in England, and the national church was based on a Presbyterian structure.

- When Charles visited Scotland for his coronation in 1633, he appears to have decided that the Presbyterian Church should be overhauled through the imposition of a hierarchical structure and English liturgy imposed.

- In 1636, Charles issued a Book of Canons, which included instructions as to how clergy should lay out their churches and introduced preaching licences. Ministers were also banned from asserting their own church rules without the king's permission.

- In 1637, Charles issued the English Prayer Book to Scottish churches. When the book was first read in St Giles Cathedral, a riot broke out.

- Disorder spread across the lowlands and in Glasgow a minister was almost killed when he was attacked by his congregation. In 1638, the Scottish clergy and nobility drew up a National Covenant to defend their religious rights. Their followers became known as Covenanters.

The First Bishops' War

Charles's quarrel with the Scots, which began with him imposing the Prayer Book in 1637, came to a head in 1639.

- Both Charles and the Covenanters raised armies. The Scottish army was far superior, and included a number of soldiers who had served the Protestant cause in the Thirty Years' War. Charles's troops lacked enthusiasm and were generally reluctant conscripts.

- Charles lacked the money to fight a war and had to rely on the part-time county militias from England.

- Realising he could not win, Charles signed the Treaty of Berwick in 1639, ending what became known as the First Bishops' War.

Ireland

When Wentworth became Lord Deputy of Ireland in 1632, he had to contend with a number of conflicting interest groups.

The Irish Parliament

Through close supervision, Wentworth was able to persuade the Irish Parliament to grant a total of ten subsidies. He also issued a new Book of Rates, which doubled incomes from customs duties. All of this revenue went directly to the English government.

The Old English

As descendants of medieval English settlers, this Catholic group had formed the elite of Irish society for two hundred years. They became aggrieved for the following reasons:

- They hated Wentworth's policy of settling English and Scottish Protestants (known as plantation) on land that once belonged to them.

- Leading Old English landowners had made an agreement with Charles known as The Graces. In return for a fixed sum, Charles promised not to interfere with certain lands. Wentworth only upheld part of the deal and did not uphold claims to land that conflicted with the Crown's interests.

The New English

More recent Protestant settlers were known as the New English. They resented Wentworth for the following reasons:

- As Protestants, they resisted the High Church Arminianism associated with Charles and Laud.

- Many of the New English had acquired vast wealth in their role as customs agents for the king, as well as through corruption. Two of the most influential members of the New English group – Richard Boyle, Earl of Cork, and Francis Annesley, Lord Mountnorris – were prosecuted in the courts by Wentworth.

Complete the paragraph   a

Below are a sample exam question and a paragraph written in answer to this question. The paragraph contains a point and specific examples, but lacks a concluding analytical link back to the question. Complete the paragraph, adding this link back to the question in the space provided.

How far was Charles I's Scottish policy responsible for the discontent towards the monarchy in the years 1629–40?

Charles's Scottish policy was extremely damaging to his reputation on both sides of the border. In 1633, he visited Scotland for his coronation and decided that the Presbyterian church system there should be reformed along Anglican lines. The fundamental problem with Charles's Scottish policy is that he misunderstood the Scots because he had spent so long in England and he had received poor guidance from his advisers. In 1636, he issued the Book of Canons and in 1637 he imposed the English Prayer Book on the Scots. This led to the formation of the National Covenant in 1638.

_____

_____

_____

Developing an argument

Below are a sample essay-style question, a list of key points to be made in the essay and a paragraph from the essay. Read the question, the plan and the sample paragraph. This supports the view put forward in the question. Rewrite the paragraph, using a similar number of words, putting forward a counter-argument. Your paragraph should explain why the situation may have been different from that put forward in the sample paragraph. When you have completed your writing, read both paragraphs. Is one or the other more convincing? Or does the truth – in your view – lie somewhere between the two claims?

To what extent were the years from 1629 to 1640 '11 years of tyranny'?

Key points

- The role of Charles's advisers
- Laud's reforms to the Church
- Religious persecution in England
- Treatment of the Scots
- Wentworth and Ireland
- Financial methods

Sample paragraph

It is clear that Charles acted in a tyrannical way in these years. In the religious sphere, both Charles and Laud were determined to impose their own vision of what the Church should be like at the expense of any who disagreed with them. Evidence of this can be found in England, where Laud took a lead role in the court of Star Chamber and punished Bastwick, Burton and Prynne harshly in 1637. The ruthless punishments they received, which included them having their ears cut off, were designed to act as an example to others. In Scotland, too, Charles imposed a new religious system based on a hierarchy of bishops on a country that had an established Presbyterian system.

The Short and Long Parliaments and the leadership of Pym, 1640–41

REVISED

The Short Parliament

The taxpayers' strike of 1639 was prompted by a lack of enthusiasm (particularly among the landowning gentry) for a war with the Scots. This meant that the most successful tax of his personal rule, Ship Money, was of no use to Charles. The London merchants only offered him £5,000 in funding because Wentworth had alienated the City of London as Lord Deputy in Ireland. He had fined the corporation of London in 1635 after it failed to fulfil its obligations towards land granted in Londonderry. This triggered a chain of events that would result in Charles assembling two hostile Parliaments.

- With finance lacking, Charles turned to Wentworth for advice. He was told to call a Parliament.
- When this so-called Short Parliament met in April 1640, numerous petitions against various aspects of personal rule, led by the MP John Pym, were presented to Charles.
- Charles had the opportunity to save the situation by making concessions to Parliament, but instead demanded money before he would hear their demands.
- Facing fierce opposition, Charles was compelled to dissolve Parliament after only three weeks.

The Second Bishops' War and the Long Parliament

Charles hastily collected together an ill-organised and under-equipped force in order to fight a second war against the Scots. Many of the soldiers he recruited actually sympathised with the Scots and stories emerged of them burning altar rails and other symbols associated with Arminianism during their march north.

The Scots easily defeated Charles's troops at the Battle of Newburn. The Treaty of Ripon was signed shortly afterwards and under its terms Charles was required to pay the Scots £850 per day while they occupied Newcastle. With all of his sources of revenue exhausted, and with new debts to pay, Charles was left with no choice but to call another Parliament. Known as the Long Parliament, it assembled in November 1640 and was not formally dissolved until March 1660.

Pym's Junto

Pym and a number of his associates, including John Hampden and Arthur Haselrig, formed the group that organised the opposition strategy to the king. Trained as a lawyer, Pym had spent much of the 1630s meticulously recording Charles's transgressions.

At the first meeting of the Long Parliament, Pym made a lengthy speech where he pushed for the 'evil councillors' to be removed. Crucially, there was no call to abolish the monarchy and no attack on Charles directly, and the opposition was in unanimous agreement that Charles's advisers were at fault and, after their removal, balance would be restored to the constitution. Shortly afterwards, William Prynne and Henry Burton – who had been imprisoned by Laud – were released from prison. Ten thousand people came out onto the streets of London to celebrate their return.

The Root and Branch Petition

In December 1640, the Commons received a Root and Branch Petition signed by 15,000 Londoners. It listed religious grievances relating to the treatment of the clergy, restrictions on preaching and the encouragement of Arminianism. It asked for the abolition of bishops, and became a blueprint for the religious policy of the opposition.

The erosion of the royal prerogative, November 1640–April 1641

Attacks on Charles's advisers

- Two of Charles's key advisers, Francis Windebank and Lord Keeper Finch, fled to the Continent in December 1640 before they could be impeached.
- The majority of judges that sat in the prerogative courts in the 1630s were impeached.
- Archbishop Laud was arrested and held in the Tower of London from November 1640. He was not executed until 1645.
- Strafford (Wentworth) was arrested and subsequently charged with high treason.

Ensuring the future security of Parliaments

- A Triennial Act was passed in February 1641. Like the Scottish version passed in 1640, it obliged Charles to call a Parliament at least once every three years. If he did not, Parliament would be able to meet anyway.
- In May 1641, Charles passed the Act Against Forcible Dissolution under enormous pressure from the London mob. According to this Act, the Long Parliament could only be dissolved with its own consent. It did not apply to future Parliaments and was therefore not a long-term restriction on the royal prerogative.

Support or challenge?

Below is a sample essay-style question which asks how far you agree with a specific statement. Below this is a series of general statements which are relevant to the question. Using your own knowledge and the information on the opposite page decide whether these statements support or challenge the statement in the question and tick the appropriate box.

How far do you agree that the main reason for the failure of personal rule was the role of Charles's advisers?

STATEMENT	SUPPORT	CHALLENGE
The Scots formed the National Covenant in 1638		
The Irish Parliament resented Charles		
Puritans were persecuted		
The taxpayers refused to pay Ship Money in 1639		
Charles decided to reform the Scottish church in 1633		
Charles relied on a number of long-forgotten taxes		
The personal stubbornness of Charles		

Develop the detail

Below is a sample essay-style question and a paragraph written in answer to this question. The paragraph contains a limited amount of detail. Annotate the paragraph to add additional detail to the answer.

'Charles's weaknesses in the Long Parliament meant that civil war was inevitable from 1640.' Assess the validity of this view.

Charles had a number of weaknesses that meant that civil war became much more likely from 1640. Because of the Second Bishops' War, Charles owed money to the Scots as they occupied Newcastle and the North East of England. He was still reliant on the same advisers that had caused problems for him in the 1630s.

Divisions and the outbreak of Civil War, 1641–42   REVISED ☐

The trial and execution of Strafford, April–May 1641

Strafford epitomised the 'evil councillors' that had apparently led Charles into errors of judgement. The details of Strafford's trial and execution are as follows:

- To be found guilty of treason, he would have to be tried in the House of Lords after a vote in the House of Commons.
- Aware that this was not possible, Pym resorted to an Act of Attainder. This was an Act of Parliament that effectively operated as a death warrant. The Act only required a suspicion of guilt, and, as long as it was passed by both Houses and signed by the monarch, no trial was required.
- To secure the passage of the Act, Pym revealed the existence of a plot by Catholic Army officers to release Strafford and dissolve Parliament by force. This became known as the First Army Plot and was followed by another at the end of 1641.
- The attainder was passed by 204 votes to 59 and Strafford was executed on 12 May. Charles agonised over signing the Attainder but eventually passed it under great pressure from Parliament and the London mob.

Other steps taken to further erode the prerogative

- In June, Tonnage and Poundage were abolished.
- In August, Ship Money was declared illegal.
- It was declared illegal for fines to be imposed in relation to knighthoods (effectively abolishing distraint of knighthood).
- Forest fines were banned.
- The Court of High Commission and the Star Chamber were outlawed due to their role in enforcing Laud's religious policies.

The Irish Rebellion, October 1641

When MPs returned to Westminster in October 1641, they were greeted by growing rumours of a rising among Irish Catholics which developed into reports of 200,000 Protestants being killed. This was grossly exaggerated.

The Grand Remonstrance, November 1641

In November, Pym introduced a lengthy document that outlined his criticisms of Charles's reign. The key points included a demand that Parliament should approve Charles's ministers and a request that Parliament have more control of the military. This was because Parliament believed that Charles could not be trusted to lead an army to quell the Irish Rebellion.

The Commons approved the Grand Remonstrance by 159 votes to 148. The closeness of the result showed that, like the country as a whole, Parliament was divided between conservatives who supported Charles and radicals who could not trust him.

In December, Arthur Haselrig presented a Militia Bill to provide an army under the control of Parliament to tackle the Irish Rebellion. This caused outraged moderates to flock to Charles's side.

The Five Members Incident

Charles now felt he was in a strong position to attack the opposition. However, this turned out to be a massive miscalculation.

- He targeted five members of the House of Commons: John Pym, John Hampden, Denzil Holles, Arthur Haselrig and William Strode. He also targeted Edward Montagu, leader of the opposition in the Lords.
- On 4 January 1642, Charles entered the Commons with an armed escort and demanded that the Speaker tell him the whereabouts of the five members. It was clear that they had already escaped as they had been forewarned of Charles's arrival.
- Charles left Parliament with nothing to show for his efforts.

The slide into war, January–August 1642

Over the course of the next few months, the chances of a settlement between the two sides did not improve and by the end of the summer they were at war.

- Fearing for the safety of his wife and children, Charles fled London on 10 January for Hampton Court and would not return to the city again as a free man.

With the gap widening between the two sides, Parliament issued a Militia Ordinance in March. This was a modified version of Haselrig's Militia Bill, but could not become law because Charles did not provide it with the royal assent. The Ordinance acted as a call to arms for Parliament, instructing lords lieutenant to raise forces in the counties. Charles responded by issuing the Commissions of Array, which also acted as a call to arms. In June, parliament issued the Nineteen Propositions as the final basis for a negotiated settlement. Again, a primary demand was an overhaul of the king's choice of ministers, but the Propositions added further requirements, such as parliamentary approval for royal tutors and future royal marriages. Unsurprisingly, Charles rejected the Propositions, arguing that anarchy would he ensue if he accepted them. In August, Charles declared war at Nottingham.

! Spot the mistake

Below are a sample essay-style question and an introductory paragraph written in answer to this question. Why does this paragraph not achieve a high level? Once you have identified the mistake, rewrite the paragraph so that it displays the qualities of a high-level essay. The mark scheme on page 5 will help you.

To what extent was the Irish Rebellion responsible for the disintegrating relationship between Charles and Parliament in the years 1625–42?

> If it was not for the Irish Rebellion, the issue of who controlled the army would not have been as important. Before the rebellion, support for the opposition cause was waning and a moderate group was emerging that felt Charles's powers had been eroded sufficiently. The rebellion caused John Pym to present the Grand Remonstrance, which included demands for the army to be controlled by Parliament. Pym now had much support, including that of the London mob who protested outside Parliament in November and December 1641.

⚡ RAG – Rate the timeline

Below is a sample exam-style question and a timeline. Read the question, study the timeline and using three coloured pens, put a red, amber or green star next to the events to show:

Red: events and policies that have no relevance to the question

Amber: events and policies that have some significance to the question

Green: events and policies that are directly relevant to the question

'Charles declared war in August 1642 because Parliament's demands were too extreme.' Explain why you agree or disagree with this view.

1629:	Beginning of personal rule
1637:	Prayer Book imposed on Scots
1639:	First Bishops' War
November 1640:	Long Parliament assembled
December 1640:	Root and Branch Petition
February 1641:	Triennial Act
May 1641:	Strafford executed
May 1641:	Act Against Forcible Dissolution
October 1641:	Irish Rebellion
November 1641:	Grand Remonstrance
January 1642:	Five Members Incident
March 1642:	Militia Ordinance
April 1642:	Charles fails to seize Hull
June 1642:	Nineteen Propositions
August 1642:	War declared

Now repeat the activity with the following question:

To what extent was Charles's personality and behaviour the primary cause of the English Civil War?

The First Civil War and reasons for Royalist defeat REVISED

Royalist weaknesses

- Although he was an enthusiastic war leader, Charles had little talent on the battlefield. He failed to capitalise on the advantages he gained in 1642 after the drawn Battle of Edgehill, where he had an opportunity to march on London.

- The Royalists were unable to secure help from abroad. Henrietta Maria landed on the Yorkshire coast in 1643 with arms and troops from Holland, but this made little impact. Charles made peace with the Irish confederates and signed the Cessation Treaty with them in the same year. This paved the way for Irish soldiers to assist Charles, but they arrived in piecemeal fashion and a weak force of 2,500 was easily defeated by Thomas Fairfax at the Battle of Nantwich in January 1644.

- Charles was unable to secure outside help because he lost control of most key ports. Newcastle and King's Lynn were the only major ports available to him in 1642, as well as a handful in the south-west.

- As he was unable to base himself in London, Charles moved his capital to Oxford. Although it was only 60 miles away from his old capital, it was far from his main supply routes to south Wales.

- Charles struggled to resolve the differences between his senior commanders. In particular, there was a damaging feud between the commander of the Royalist cavalry, Prince Rupert, who was Charles's nephew, and Lord Digby.

- Money from traditional levies soon ran out and it was not until 1644 that Charles emulated Parliament in instituting an excise tax.

Parliamentarian strengths

- Parliament controlled London, the capital and the city with the largest population. London contained the printing presses that would assist in a widespread propaganda campaign and the blacksmiths and tailors that supplied the army.

- The strongest militia in 1642 – the London trained bands – numbered 20,000 men by 1643. They had been highly trained and funded since the 1630s, and were drilled by professional soldiers.

- Controlling London gave the Parliamentarians access to loans and funding from the City of London merchants.

- Political legitimacy was associated with the control of Parliament itself. Parliament's representatives were able to effectively administer the various government departments formerly managed by Charles's councillors.

- Parliament controlled the navy and most of the ports (including London). This made it difficult for Charles to obtain help from the Continent.

- The south and east of England, controlled by Parliament, were the wealthiest and most agriculturally rich regions in the country. When their effective tax regime was implemented this meant that they were able to raise much more revenue than Charles, and grain from the south-east fed the army.

- The political leadership of Parliament was relatively strong and united in 1642 and 1643, before the death of John Pym.

Divisions amongst the parliamentary leaders and the Self-Denying Ordinance

Parliament won the Battle of Marston Moor in July 1644 with Scottish help, but, at the Second Battle of Newbury in October 1644, Parliament failed to achieve victory despite outnumbering the king's army by more than two to one. Cautious tactics from the Earl of Manchester, a member of the 'Peace' faction (who wanted a negotiated settlement with the king), were responsible. Oliver Cromwell and other members of the 'War' party (who wanted to push on to complete victory and impose a settlement on Charles) passed the Self-Denying Ordinance in 1644. This necessitated all MPs and Lords to resign their military commands. This was intended to remove commanders who had performed poorly, such as the Earl of Essex and the Earl of Manchester, with whom Cromwell had a personal disagreement after Newbury. The Ordinance was revised in April 1645 to allow some MPs to be reappointed. Cromwell himself was thus recalled.

The formation of the New Model Army

In February 1645, an ordinance was passed creating the New Model Army. The Army was unique for a number of reasons.

- It was a single national force of 21,000 men.

- Members were well paid, with infantry receiving eightpence per day.

- Promotions were based on merit rather than social class.

- Members of the Army were deeply religious, and genuinely believed they were fighting a just war in the name of God.

- All infantry wore the same (red) uniform.

- Discipline was strict and soldiers could be fined for swearing.

- The Army contained an intelligence department responsible for collecting information about enemy movements.

Quick quizzes at www.hoddereducation.co.uk/myrevisionnotes

Mind map

Use the information on the opposite page to add detail to the mind map below to help understand the reasons behind Parliamentary victory.

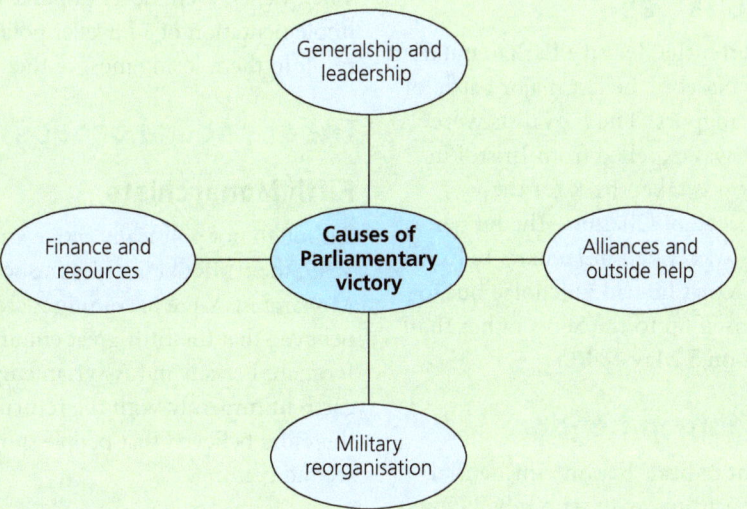

Developing an argument

Below are a sample A-level exam-style question, a list of key points to be made in the essay and a paragraph from the essay. Read the question, the plan and the sample paragraph. Rewrite the paragraph in order to develop an argument. Your paragraph should explain why the factor discussed in the paragraph is either the most significant factor or less significant than another factor.

'Parliament's victory in the Civil War was the most important reason why it was difficult to find a political settlement in the years 1629–46.' How far do you agree with this view?

Key points

- Reasons for Parliament's victory in the Civil War, including New Model Army
- Finance
- Religious issues
- Conflicts with Parliament

Sample paragraph

The New Model Army was a professional fighting force not seen before in England. The soldiers were well trained, paid regularly and had religious zeal. They were also subject to harsh discipline and could be fined for swearing. They all wore the same uniform and had many of the same beliefs. The Army believed that God was on their side and would sing psalms before going into battle.

Social divisions and the emergence of political and religious radicalism

REVISED

The capture of Charles

In July 1645, a month after the decisive Parliamentarian victory at the Battle of Naseby, the last major battle of the war took place at Langport. The Royalists were easily defeated. Rupert was expelled from Bristol in September and the city was taken back for the Parliamentarians. The siege of Chester – the longest of the war at 15 months – was ended in January 1646. By now, Charles was aware that he had no choice but to surrender. He gave himself up to the Scots rather than the English Parliament on 5 May 1646.

Popular radicalism in London

A number of prominent radicals became influential towards the end of the war, many of whom had close links to the Army. The radical Puritan and soldier John Lilburne was imprisoned in 1645 for denouncing MPs who continued to live in comfort while soldiers died on the battlefield. He was defended by William Walwyn, who advocated complete religious freedom and toleration for all. Walwyn collaborated with another London radical, Richard Overton, to organise a petition for Lilburne's release.

Lilburne and the Levellers

Beliefs

The Leveller movement emerged in 1645. Levellers became particularly influential in the aftermath of the Civil War, and they developed their own plans for a written constitution, *An Agreement of the People*, between 1647 and 1649. Overall, the Leveller demands consisted of the following:

- The abolition of the House of Lords to make the House of Commons the central body in the political system.
- Universal male suffrage.
- A new written constitution.
- Equality before the law and religious freedom.

Impact

The Levellers were undoubtedly revolutionary, as they demanded a complete overhaul of the political and legal system, the vote for every man and an end to imprisonment for debt. However, they did not advocate bringing women into the voting franchise, and some Levellers suggested those receiving poor relief should not vote. The fact that Parliament imprisoned Lilburne for his beliefs in 1645 suggests that they were viewed as a threat.

Their beliefs were never popular with the gentry as the implementation of a Leveller political programme would result in them losing most of their power.

Other radical groups

Fifth Monarchists

Although not politically active and influential until after 1649, the millenarian ideas associated with the Fifth Monarchists were becoming increasingly popular. They believed that the fifth great empire (after the Greek, Roman, Persian and Assyrian empires) would come to earth imminently with the return of Jesus. Millenarians therefore believed that people should prepare for the second coming.

Ranters

A small group of preachers, calling themselves Ranters, appeared in London around this time. Contemporary pamphlets about the Ranters claimed they argued that those predestined to be saved by God were incapable of sin and could therefore ignore man-made codes of social morality. They believed, therefore, that immoral sexual behaviour, drinking, swearing and crime were legitimate activities. There is, however, doubt about whether they were a significant force or whether they even existed at all. Sources discussing the Ranters were all written by their natural enemies, those conservatives who would benefit from a population too fearful to stray away from the Protestant path.

Diggers

The Diggers, or True Levellers, were led by Gerard Winstanley and were equally scandalous in the eyes of the Political Nation. They claimed that the ownership of land was based on man-made laws and that there was no evidence in the Bible to suggest they should be followed. They set up rural communes for the poor on common land.

Mind map

Use the information on the opposite page to add detail to the mind map below to help understand the radicalism of the late 1640s.

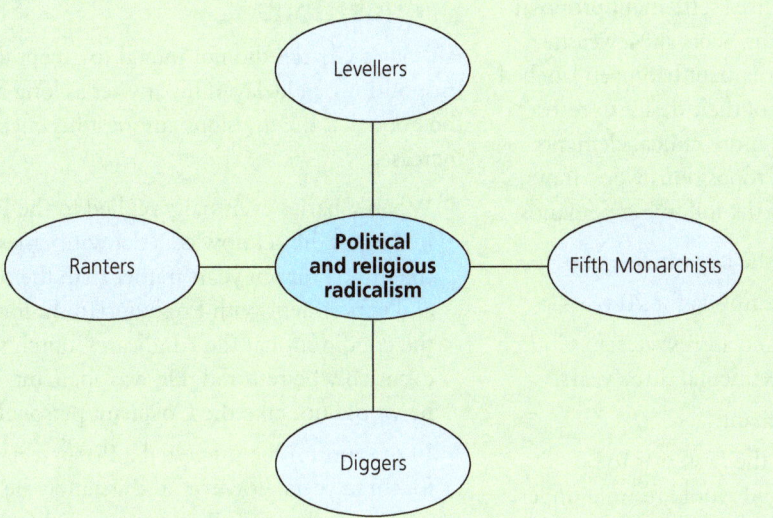

 Use own knowledge to support or contradict a

Below is an extract to read. You are asked to summarise the interpretation about the Levellers and then develop a counter-argument.

Interpretation offered by the source:

_____

_____

Counter-argument:

_____

_____

_____

_____

EXTRACT A

From I. Gentles, J. Morrill and B. Worden, Soldiers, Writers and Statesmen of the English Revolution *(2008).*

On one view the Levellers were so socially conservative, so limited in their democratic desires, that they differed little if at all from the later seventeenth-century 'Commonswealthmen' and the more radical of the early Whigs. Their contemporaries misunderstood them, or to put it another way they appeared to be more radical than they really were, partly through inadvertence [accident], partly due to their tactical ineptitude... those who were given the name Levellers by their enemies were open to portrayal as dangerous extremists, whether in good faith... or disingenuously in order to discredit them.

The search for a settlement, 1646–47

The Newcastle Propositions

Parliament offered Charles an initial settlement proposal while he was in the custody of the Scots at Newcastle. The group now dominating Parliament had been labelled 'political Presbyterians' because of their desire to restrict religious freedom and bring the more radical elements under control. The Newcastle Propositions were drawn up in July 1646 and consisted of the following demands:

- Parliament would nominate the key officers of state.
- Parliament would control the militia for 20 years.
- Bishops would be abolished and a Presbyterian Church would be created for an experimental three years.
- Charles was to sign the Covenant.
- The king's peace treaty with the Irish was to be annulled and the war in Ireland would resume under the command of Parliament.
- Fifty-eight Royalists were to be exempt from pardon and punished for their involvement in the Civil War.

Charles handed to the English

The Scots soon came to realise that their prisoner would not agree to their demands for him to implement a fully Presbyterian Church of England. There was also resentment from English MPs, which was exacerbated when an intercepted letter revealed that Charles had been in secret negotiations with the Scots since the beginning of 1646. When it became clear that Charles was not going to agree to any peace treaties in the immediate future, the English paid the Scots for custody of Charles. The Scots left England in January 1647 and Charles was held at Holmby House in Northamptonshire.

Charles's attitude to the Newcastle Propositions

Even before he received a copy of the Newcastle Propositions, Charles was aware of their probable content and always vowed that he would not accept them. He believed that a Presbyterian church would irreparably damage the power of the monarchy because obedience to the Crown had never been associated with the Presbyterian Church in Scotland. Letters sent to Henrietta Maria before the Propositions had been formally presented show that Charles never intended to negotiate, and stated that if he accepted them he would lose his 'conscience, crown and honour'.

Charles's response to the Newcastle Propositions

Although Charles did not intend to accept the Propositions, he delayed his answer as long as possible in the hope that the divisions amongst his enemies would increase.

- When Charles eventually replied to the Propositions in August, he acknowledged a willingness to surrender the militia for ten years (rather than the suggested 20) and experiment with Presbyterianism for five years, on the condition that the Anglican Church would eventually be restored. He was adamant, however, that he would not take the Covenant personally.
- In the autumn he suggested a Presbyterian settlement for three years; however, the assembly he proposed would consist of 20 Presbyterians, 20 Independents (who believed each congregation should function entirely separately) and 20 of his own nominees.
- He was advised by some of his counsellors, including Henrietta Maria, that he should make concessions on the issue of Church governance but both this issue and control of the militia were non-negotiable for Charles.
- In May 1647, he offered to accept a modified version of the Propositions with Presbyterianism implemented for three years. He did this as he was already considering raising a Scottish army to help him regain the throne and was also considering continuing the war with French assistance. The revolt of the New Model Army shortly afterwards meant that any negotiations had to be delayed.

Complete the paragraph

Below are a sample exam-style question and a paragraph written in answer to this question. The paragraph contains a point and specific examples but lacks a concluding explanatory link back to the question. Complete the paragraph, adding this link in the space provided.

'Charles I was personally responsible for the lack of a political settlement in the years 1629–49'. Assess the validity of this view.

Charles never intended to make a settlement with Parliament after the Civil War as he still believed he could achieve ultimate victory. He remained the legitimate monarch and he was aware that it would be impossible to make any kind of settlement without him on the throne. He was also well aware that his enemies, including Parliament and the Scots, were divided amongst themselves. When he was offered the Newcastle Propositions in July 1646 he deliberately delayed his answer in the hope that the divisions in Parliament would widen and he would be welcomed back on similar terms to those in which he ruled the country formerly.

_____

_____

Support or challenge?

Below is a sample exam-style question which asks how far you agree with a specific statement. Below this is a series of general statements which are relevant to the question. Using your own knowledge and the information on the opposite page decide whether these statements support or challenge the statement in the question and tick the appropriate box.

How far do you agree that the main reason for the failure of a political settlement in the years 1629–49 was disagreements over religion?

STATEMENT	SUPPORT	CHALLENGE
The English Prayer Book was imposed on the Scots		
Pym issued the Grand Remonstrance		
The New Model Army was created in 1645		
The Newcastle Propositions were issued to Charles in 1646		
Charles rejected the Newcastle Propositions		
Laud was appointed Archbishop of Canterbury in 1633		

Divisions in the army, 1647

Presbyterians and Independents

The two groups that emerged in Parliament initially had conflicting views about a future religious settlement.

Presbyterian beliefs

Like the Scots, this group of MPs wanted to abolish episcopacy and replace it with a Presbyterian system. There would still be a national church but the hierarchy of bishops would be replaced with an assembly. Their chief spokesperson was Denzil Holles, who was involved in writing the Newcastle Propositions. Politically, this group favoured a negotiated settlement with Charles and the prompt disbanding of the New Model Army.

Independent beliefs

Instead of a single national church, the independents believed that each Christian congregation should be autonomous. This group was a minority in Parliament but had a number of powerful supporters, including Oliver Cromwell and Lord Saye and Sele. Politically, they wanted to force a settlement on the king rather than continue with protracted negotiations.

The extent of divisions, 1647

Despite the fact that the Presbyterians were the largest and most dominant group in Parliament, as Charles delayed his response to the Newcastle Propositions throughout 1646 and into 1647, their position became weaker. The balance of power now shifted between the Presbyterians and Independents.

- Seats in the House of Commons that had become vacant were filled by 'recruiter' elections. Many of these were won by Independents.
- The Presbyterians were boosted when Charles was transferred to their custody in January 1647.
- The Independents in Parliament had close links to the New Model Army. The Presbyterians planned to disband much of the Army with only eight weeks' arrears of pay (they were owed £3 million) and send 12,000 of them to Ireland. In March 1647, the House of Commons voted that only Presbyterian and non-MPs should serve as officers. The Army, backed by the Independents, refused on 29 May.
- One issue that both factions were in relative agreement over was the threat of radicals such as the Levellers. In early 1647, the Levellers became increasingly active in London. They issued a petition in March stating that the nation was still oppressed and their grievances had not changed. The House of Commons, with significant backing from the Independent MPs, ordered the petition to be burned.

The Army revolt, June 1647

On 4 June, a junior officer, Cornet Joyce, arrived with an escort at Holmby House to take possession of the king, effectively kidnapping him from the custody of the Presbyterians. This triggered a significant chain of events.

- Charles was taken to join the Army at Newmarket, from where he was transferred to his old royal palace at Hampton Court.
- The next day, leading officers (including Cromwell) signed an Engagement to stand with the Army.
- A General Council of the Army was established, consisting of both officers and Agitators. The Council met to discuss political issues including their grievances against the Presbyterian MPs.
- In mid-June, the *Representation of the Army* was published, written by Cromwell's son-in-law, Henry Ireton. In it, he demanded the expulsion of 11 Presbyterian MPs and fresh elections with a wider electorate.
- Fifty-eight Independent MPs and peers sought refuge with the Army and Fairfax led his forces into London on 4 August.
- The Army deliberately marched through London in a show of strength and Fairfax was appointed Constable of the Tower of London. Six of the 11 Presbyterian MPs named by the Independents then fled abroad.

The Heads of the Proposals

It is clear that by mid-August 1647, the Independents and the Army were in a position of strength. During the initial stages of the Army revolt, there was considerable unity between officers and rank-and-file soldiers. This changed when Ireton presented Charles with a new offer for a political settlement, the Heads of the Proposals. It included the following clauses:

- The Triennial Act would be repealed and replaced with Biennial Parliaments.
- Parliament would nominate key officers of state for ten years.
- Parliament would control the militia for ten years.
- There would be continued use of bishops in the Church of England but a restriction on their coercive powers.
- Seven Royalists were to be exempt from pardon, rather than the 58 included in the Newcastle Propositions.

The Heads of the Proposals were more reasonable to Charles than the Newcastle Propositions. He now accepted these as his favoured settlement proposals. The Army grandees now appeared as a moderate force who were willing to reinstate Charles with most of his powers intact.

Mind map

Use the information on the opposite page to add detail to the mind map below in order to develop your understanding of the attempts to reach a political settlement.

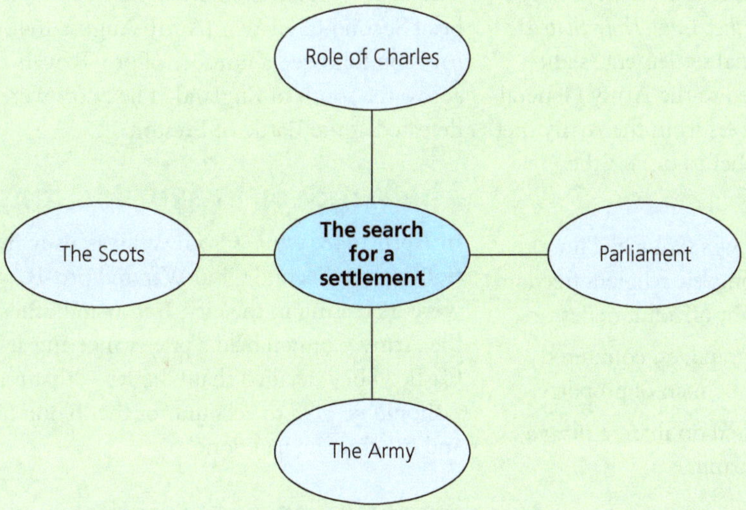

Developing an argument

Below are a sample essay-style question, a list of key points to be made in the essay and a paragraph from the essay. Read the question, the plan and the sample paragraph. This supports the view put forward in the question. Rewrite the paragraph, using a similar number of words, putting forward a counter-argument. Your paragraph should explain why the situation may have been different from that put forward in the sample paragraph. When you have completed your writing, read both paragraphs. Is one or the other more convincing? Or does the truth – in your view – lie somewhere between the two claims?

To what extent were radicals in the New Model Army responsible for the failure to reach a political settlement in the years 1645–48?

Key points

- Radicals and Agitators in the Army
- Divisions in Parliament
- The role of the Army grandees
- The actions of Charles

Sample paragraph

In early 1647 it looked as though a political settlement with Charles was close. The Newcastle Propositions were reasonably moderate and Charles had suggested that he was prepared to accept a modified version of them in order to bring him back to power. The Army were unhappy with the fact that they were owed £3 million in arrears of pay and they feared they would be left out of a political settlement, despite their sacrifices. In April 1647 they began to elect Agitators to represent their views and in June Cornet Joyce kidnapped the king. This represented a key turning point in the search for a settlement because not only were there divisions within Parliament but there were now divisions between the some of the leaders of the Independent faction and the rank-and-file soldiers.

The Second Civil War and Regicide, 1648–49

The Putney Debates

In October 1647, the Leveller-influenced soldiers offered their own proposals in the *Case of the Army Truly Stated*, which was drawn up into a potential settlement as *An Agreement of the People* and presented to the Army General Council. Agitators and senior officers from the Army met at a church in Putney in late October to discuss the political settlement.

- The spokesman for the radicals was Colonel Thomas Rainsborough. He demanded complete religious freedom and annual Parliaments elected by all adult males.
- Ireton, speaking for the Army grandees, countered with the claim that voters must be men of property.
- Cromwell was present but focused on maintaining a level of civility between participants.

The Engagement and the role of the Scots

Charles's escape

The Putney Debates were brought to an abrupt end by the news that Charles had escaped from captivity at Hampton Court. He was soon in custody again at Carisbrooke Castle on the Isle of Wight but again attempted to escape several times, on one occasion becoming wedged between some window bars and having to use a candle to signal to his supporters on the outside that he was stuck.

The Corkbush Field mutiny

Charles's escape signalled the end of the Putney Debates and the Agitators had to return to their regiments. At one army muster at Corkbush Field, near Ware in Hertfordshire, a group of radicals appeared with copies of *An Agreement of the People*. Cromwell quickly rode into the ranks to restore order and punish their leaders, one of whom was shot.

The Engagement

While on the Isle of Wight, Charles was approached by envoys from Scotland. He was offered the Engagement, which he promptly accepted on 26 December, while rejecting Parliament's Four Bills (a modified version of the Newcastle Propositions). In return for military assistance from the Scots, Charles agreed to establish a Presbyterian Church in England for three years.

Vote of No Addresses

On 3 January 1648, the House of Commons passed the Vote of No Addresses by 141 votes to 91. It stated that no more negotiations would be held with Charles because of his negotiations with the Scots. The House of Lords initially refused to debate the issue but passed it on 17 January.

Charles defeated

The Scots entered England in April 1648, triggering the brief Second Civil War (April–August 1648). This invasion followed a number of pro-Royalist protests across the south of England. The Scots were easily defeated at the Battle of Preston.

The Windsor Prayer Meeting

In April 1648, while Cromwell was away from London fighting the Second Civil War and pro-Royalist riots were increasing in the city, Ireton and other officers from the Army Council held a prayer meeting at Windsor Castle. They decided that Charles – 'that man of blood' – should be held to account for the 'blood he had shed, and mischief he had done'.

Negotiations at Newport

Ireton petitioned Parliament several times over the next few months in the hope of organising a trial. Parliament, however, attempted one more round of negotiations with Charles and in August discussions began at Newport. Charles resorted to his old tactics of deception and delay.

Pride's Purge

The view that Charles should be brought to trial was still that of a minority into early December 1648. In the early hours of 5 December Parliament voted to continue negotiations with Charles. The next day, a regiment led by Colonel Thomas Pride surrounded the House of Commons and excluded 186 MPs who supported continued negotiations and arrested another 45. This left a 'Rump' House of 240, of whom 71 would become actively involved in the trial and execution of Charles.

The trial

With Cromwell finally in agreement with Ireton that Charles should be brought to trial, the House of Commons issued an ordinance creating a special court to hold the trial on 1 January 1649. The Lords rejected this. The Commons then declared that it had sole authority to pass laws without king or Lords. They passed an Act to set up a High Court of Justice and Charles's trial took place on 20–27 January. One hundred and thirty five commissioners were appointed and 68 heard the case, including Cromwell and Ireton. Throughout the trial Charles refused to recognise the authority of the court and he was found guilty of treason. He was publicly beheaded outside his old Banqueting House at Whitehall on 30 January.

RAG – Rate the timeline

Below is a sample essay question and a timeline. Read the question, study the timeline and using three coloured pens, put a red, amber or green star next to the events to show:

Red: events and policies that have no relevance to the question

Amber: events and policies that have some significance to the question

Green: events and policies that are directly relevant to the question

'Charles was personally responsible for the failure to reach a political settlement in the years 1646–49.' Explain why you agree or disagree with this view.

July 1646:	The Newcastle Propositions presented to Charles; Charles sends letters to his wife stating that he will not yield to any demands
January 1647:	The Scots leave England and Charles is kept in the custody of the Presbyterians
April 1647:	The New Model Army elect Agitators
May 1647:	Charles offered to accept a modified version of the Newcastle Propositions after delaying his answer
June 1647:	Cornet Joyce seizes Charles, triggering the Army revolt
July 1647:	Presbyterians storm Parliament
August 1647:	The Heads of the Proposals presented to the king
October 1647:	The Putney Debates
November 1647:	Charles escapes from Hampton Court and subsequently signs the Engagement with the Scots
January 1648:	Vote of No Addresses
April 1648:	Second Civil War; Windsor Prayer Meeting
August 1648:	Renewed negotiations begin at Newport
December 1648:	Pride's Purge
January 1649:	Trial and execution

Now repeat the activity with the following question:

To what extent was Charles I executed because of the influence of the Levellers?

Recommended reading

Below is a list of suggested further reading on this topic.

- *Charles I*, pages 420–66, Richard Cust (2007)
- *Killers of the King: The Men Who Dared to Execute Charles I*, pages 3–29, Charles Spencer (2015)
- *A Brief History of the English Civil Wars*, pages 141–203, John Miller (2009)

Exam focus (AS-level)

Below is a sample Level 4 answer to an AS-style question on interpretations. Read it and the comments around it.

With reference to Extracts A and B and your understanding of the historical context, which of these two extracts provides the more convincing interpretation of the reasons for the execution of Charles I?

EXTRACT A

From B. Coward, The Stuart Age *(2011).*

The English Revolution – the purge of parliament in December 1648 and the trial and execution of the king in January 1649 – was carried out by a tiny clique against the wishes of the vast majority in the country... The fact that the events of December 1648 to January 1649 were carried out by a minority drawn largely from outside the traditional ruling elite in England and against the wishes of that elite goes a long way towards explaining the eventual failure of the new English republic. Yet, paradoxically, the history of the republic confirms that only a limited political revolution had taken place 1648–9, and one that was reversed in 1660. The basic structure of society remained unaffected. But it is surely semantic quibbling to deny the unique revolutionary nature of the abolition of the episcopacy, monarchy and the House of Lords... if there ever has been an English Revolution, it surely took place from December 1648 to January 1649.

EXTRACT B

From B. Worden, The English Civil War, 1640–1660 *(2009).*

The longer the war had lasted, the deeper the conflicts within parliament and among its followers had become. In politics the division was between a war party, which wanted to bring the king to his knees and impose a settlement on him, and a peace party, which wanted him restored by negotiation... The impact of the Levellers on the soldiers, which had initially worked to the advantage of the Cromwellians, had by the autumn come to threaten the new model's unity. Cromwell and Ireton were accused by their subordinates of selling out to the king in their negotiations with him, and of failing to insist on the army's demands for reform. In November a mutiny at Ware in Hertfordshire was vigorously suppressed, and the machinery of wide consultation and debate within the new model was terminated.

While both extracts appear to give good interpretations of the reasons for the execution of Charles I, it seems Extract B gives the more convincing interpretation.

This is because it references the more long-term reasons for the execution, rather than focusing solely on the actions of the minority who put Charles on trial. The extract mentions 'the impact of the Levellers on the soldiers'. This impact appears to be vital in understanding the execution. The Levellers were the first group to push for the execution of the king, and their manifesto, *An Agreement of the People*, advocated the abolition of the monarchy and the House of Lords, as well as the vote for every man. These radical ideas undoubtedly had an impact on those who ultimately executed Charles, meaning that the extract provides an accurate interpretation of the events.

It is also clear that the interpretation of the events given in Extract B is accurate because it mentions the divisions that existed in Parliament between 'the war party that wanted to bring the king to his knees', and the peace party that wanted to restore him. These divisions contributed to the execution of Charles because they encouraged him to delay his answer to the Newcastle Propositions in 1646 and 1647 in the hope that his enemies would become so divided amongst themselves that they would call for his return to the throne with his original powers intact. The war party supporters were closely associated with the New Model Army, and when the Army revolted in June 1647 they expelled a number of Presbyterians from Parliament and seized the city.

This is a sensible opening, but could be improved by making a fully substantiated judgement about the relative usefulness of the two extracts.

This paragraph features good contextual knowledge to corroborate the extract, but could be more detailed.

Focus on another issue brought out of the extract, with strong factual knowledge used in support.

However, it could be argued that the source isn't accurate in its interpretation in that it could be seen that the Levellers actually had very little influence on the final decision to execute Charles. For example, the Levellers had very radical ideas but the people who decided to kill the king were members of the gentry who would never be interested in following these ideas. This means that the execution was more likely influenced by the actions of the small minority headed by Cromwell and Ireton. Cromwell himself was torn between his religious convictions and immediate political concerns, and was initially indecisive because he wanted to wait for God to clarify the way forward. This means that the extract may not be providing a convincing interpretation of the events surrounding the execution.

Balance introduced with limitations of Extract B. However, there is limited knowledge on what the Levellers believed.

On the other hand, though, it could be argued that Extract A provides a less convincing interpretation of the reasons for the execution.

Extract A describes the execution as having been carried out by a 'tiny clique' against the wishes of the rest of the population. There is plenty of evidence to support this view. It is true that it is only when Charles had shown his duplicity by signing the Engagement with the Scots in December 1647 that the senior members of the Army decided that regicide might be an option. Charles started the Second Civil War by doing this, and Ireton took part in the Windsor Prayer Meeting in April 1648, where it was decided that Charles, 'that man of blood', should be brought to trial for his crimes. Cromwell only became involved in the decision at a very late stage and no one really knows exactly why.

This paragraph begins to analyse Extract A and provides sound knowledge to corroborate it. More could be included on Cromwell's role.

Extract A also proves to be a convincing interpretation when it speaks about those who killed Charles coming from 'outside the traditional ruling elite'. This can be evidenced through the fact that Cromwell and Ireton, as well as the other leading Army officers and the judge at the trial (John Bradshaw) were from the gentry class. Many of the higher nobility had supported Charles and some historians suggest that the Civil War and ultimately the execution were the result of a gentry coup against royal authority.

This paragraph highlights the issue of class but could be more developed.

However, it could be argued that Extract A is not providing a convincing interpretation of the events because it only references the events of December 1648 and January 1649, and does not look to long-term factors that were clearly responsible for the decision to execute the king. There is no mention of the debates between Charles and Parliament, or the internal arguments within the Army that led to the Putney Debates in October 1647. This means that Extract A is not an accurate portrayal of the events because it does not present a range of factors.

This paragraph highlights the evidence that is missing from the extract.

Finally, it could be argued that Extract A is not an accurate portrayal of the reasons for execution because it neglects the role of Charles in the trial. He remained stubborn throughout the proceedings and refused to acknowledge the legitimacy of the court. He claimed that no court had the right to put a monarch on trial, and certainly not for high treason. He also claimed that it was not possible for a monarch to commit treason.

The conclusion asserts rather than argues and could be more developed.

Overall, it appears Extract B is more accurate because it presents long-term factors and covers much of the vital context to the trial that Extract A does not assess.

The answer is generally effective in approach, in that it seeks both to corroborate and challenge the arguments and reach a conclusion as to which is the more convincing, although the conclusion is assertive. It is more effective in its treatment of Extract B, where the knowledge cited is more relevant and appropriate. The treatment of Extract A is confused and limited. The answer tends to select arguments which are more easily challenged and corroborated, but does not provide a clear understanding of the overall arguments in each extract. This has the qualities of a low Level 4 overall.

What makes a good answer?

List the characteristics of a good interpretations-based answer, using the examples and comments above.

Exam focus (A-level)

Below is a sample Level 5 answer to an A-level style question on interpretations. Read it and the comments around it.

Using your understanding of the historical context, assess how convincing the arguments in Extracts A and B on page 46 and Extract C below are in relation to the reasons for the execution of Charles I.

EXTRACT C

From G.E. Aylmer, The Struggle for the Constitution, 1603–1689 *(1968).*

It has often been said that Charles I died a martyr for the Church of England, that it was his unshakable defence of his Anglican principles and his refusal to compromise or surrender these, which led to his judicial murder by the extreme Puritans. This argument is not very convincing. More than once during the torturous negotiations of 1646–8, Charles had agreed to accept a Presbyterian system for a longish period. His apologists might argue that this was done in bad faith, but if so, it is strange that he did not lie consistently, and so survive to continue his duplicity after 1649... Rising to the occasion, Charles faced his death with more dignity and good sense than he had often shown in his life. Yet for all this, he cannot truly be said to have stood for the laws and liberties of the country... Remembering the 1630s, let alone his activities in the mid- and late 1640s, it is impossible to picture Charles as a sincere constitutional ruler.

Clearly, Charles was executed for a number of reasons, including the influence of radical Levellers in the Army and the divisions amongst the opposition. However, his own duplicity and his previous unwillingness to negotiate adequately was the paramount reason.

Therefore, the argument put forward in Extract C is the most convincing of the three. Extract A argues that the execution took place because of the actions of a small group of senior Army officers. Extract B continues by emphasising the importance of the Army, but highlights the divisions that existed in the opposition.

> The opening statement is assertive and sets out the conclusion reached. However, it would be better to relate the assertions to particular extracts. Note that 'most' is not actually asked for in the question, so an assessment of each Extract is needed.

The argument put forward in Extract C discusses both Charles's attempts to reach a sensible negotiated peace and the behaviour that caused the Civil War in the first place. It states that it is impossible to see him as a 'sincere constitutional ruler', and there is much evidence to support this view. Charles broke with precedent many times during his rule, starting when he collected Tonnage and Poundage without the consent of Parliament in the 1620s and 30s. His collection of prerogative taxes such as Ship Money, which raised £200,000 a year in the 1630s, also shows that he was prepared to break with constitutional convention. The Extract does, however, claim that Charles attempted to make a settlement with Parliament after the Civil War and accepted 'a Presbyterian system for a longish period'. This is partially true, as Charles's answer to the Newcastle Propositions suggested that he would accept a reformed Church. However, he sent letters to his wife stating that he was prepared to delay his answer for as long as possible in order to disrupt negotiations. In essence, the Extract does much to advance our understanding of the execution because it highlights some of the behaviours exhibited by Charles that ultimately led to his downfall.

> This paragraph successfully assesses the argument put forward in Extract C. It uses contextual knowledge well to both corroborate and refute the claims made in the Extract.

Despite the weight given to the failures of Charles in Extract C, divisions amongst the opposition and in particular, the actions of the Levellers, cannot be ignored when attempting to explain the reasons for the execution. Extract B highlights the influence that the Levellers had on the New Model Army, and it is clear that many of the demands made by the Army had Leveller influence. The original demands of the Army in the summer of 1647 were for arrears of pay (they were owed £3 million), but they soon changed to demands for political reform and attacks on the Presbyterian faction in Parliament.

> The focus here is on the issues brought out of Extract B, and the paragraph ultimately concludes that it is not a very convincing interpretation with a full justification.

The war party in Parliament generally supported the Army, and the Extract mentions the divisions in Parliament but does not give them much weight in explaining the final decision to execute the king. What ultimately paved the way for the execution of the king was the actions of the Army after Charles started the Second Civil War in 1648, and despite the fact that Extract B states that 'the longer the war had lasted, the deeper the conflicts within Parliament and among its followers had become', this was now irrelevant as there was more of a consensus that something should be done with Charles. On balance, Extract B is therefore limited in gaining a complete insight into the reasons for the execution.

The unconstitutional actions of Charles mentioned in relation to Extract C, as well as his responsibility for causing the Second Civil War, led senior Army officers such as Ireton to make the decision that he should be executed. This 'tiny clique' – as they are referred to in Extract A – formed a High Court of Justice to try Charles without being granted any judicial authority. It is true that Charles was probably more popular at the moment of his death than he had ever been, so this opinion bears a lot of weight. However, the events would not have played out as they did if it was not for the actions of Charles, making the Extract less convincing. The most significant member of this clique was Oliver Cromwell, who only agreed with the decision to put the king on trial at the last minute. He was from the group outside 'the traditional ruling elite' referred to in the Extract, and the vast majority of those who signed the death warrant were from the gentry class rather than the nobility. In focusing solely on the small group that executed Charles, the author fails to acknowledge the more deep-rooted differences between the king and opposition, and Charles's many transgressions, such as his escape from Hampton Court (which prematurely ended the Putney Debates and any hope of the Levellers being satisfied) are not included.

> Good understanding of the argument in Extract A shown, with relevant knowledge deployed to assist in assessing it.

In conclusion, the most convincing explanation for why Charles was executed is provided in Extract C. While it is true that the group of Army officers who arranged the trial were important, it could be argued that their role was only necessarily because of the way events had played out over the previous two years. In addition, while the Levellers were an important force for a time, their influence became relatively redundant after the Putney Debates, when the Army officers increased their stranglehold over the military. Rather, the best explanation that explains why Charles was executed comes from the king himself, in both his long-term policies and his short-term behaviour.

> The concluding paragraph is not needed, because an overall judgement is not asked for (and is not there in the mark scheme). In fact it does not add anything significant to what has been argued already in the answer.

A very good answer: the arguments of the extracts are clearly identified and knowledge of context is used to corroborate and challenge the arguments in clear and appropriate detail.

The conclusion is not needed or expected.

This is a Level 5 response, but the limited challenge to Extract C places the response more to the middle of the level rather than the top.

Exam focus

One of the reasons why this essay is successful is that it maintains a strong focus on the question. There is a lot of detail on the role of the different groups responsible for Charles's execution. Go through the essay and underline every mention of either key individuals or key groups involved. Next, look at an essay you have written and underline your use of key words. Can you improve your own efforts in light of what you have seen here?

3 From republic to restored and limited monarchy, 1649–78

The consolidation of the republic, 1649–51

Rump government

Those who carried out the execution of Charles faced problems in establishing a government to replace him. Ireland was a Royalist stronghold and Charles II was immediately declared king in Scotland in February 1649. The Rump now tasked itself with removing the last vestiges of Royalism from England.

- The Rump declared that it had sole legislative authority.
- It elected the Council of State, which acted as a government council similar to the Privy Council.
- In March 1649, the monarchy and House of Lords were abolished.
- In May, England was declared to be a 'Commonwealth and free state', governed by a single-chamber Parliament.

The Third Civil War and foreign policy

No foreign monarchies were prepared to recognise the legitimacy of the Rump after it had executed Charles. In a time of such uncertainty, the navy was bolstered by the construction of 20 new warships. This navy provided much needed support for Cromwell's expedition to Ireland and the Third Civil War against the Royalist Scots.

Ireland

Cromwell, with 20,000 men, landed in Ireland in August 1649 to suppress Catholic Royalist sympathisers. Rebellious forces had controlled Ireland since the initial uprising in 1641. Cromwell expected a swift victory but only achieved success after he had stormed the strongholds of Drogheda and Wexford, controversially slaughtering thousands of defenders after they had surrendered. As so often in his military career, he justified the massacre by referring to it as Divine Providence.

Scotland

Cromwell returned to England in 1650 to conquer Scotland, leaving Ireton to complete the Irish campaign. Although they had been Parliament's allies, the Scots had cut ties with the English after Charles's execution. After Charles II was declared king in Scotland and made peace with the Covenanters, they assembled an army to invade England. With Fairfax reluctant to take on the task of marching to Scotland to attack first, Cromwell was appointed Commander-in-Chief and the Third Civil War began. Two major battles define the war.

- After marching to Scotland with 15,000 men, in September 1650, Cromwell defeated the Scots at Dunbar.
- Charles led his army south a year later, hoping to gain support, but his dispirited troops were defeated by Cromwell at Worcester on 3 September 1651.

Charles escaped to the Continent after famously hiding in an oak tree to avoid detection. He spent the next nine years in exile in France and later in the United Provinces, before the Restoration in 1660. The Rump was now in control of all parts of the British Isles.

The Dutch

The United Provinces was a Protestant state and one of the few to recognise the Rump from early 1651. Despite the potential for the Dutch and English to become allies, the passing of the Navigation Act in 1651 resulted in anger from the Dutch. The Dutch received much of their revenue from transatlantic trade and the inability to use English ports had a detrimental impact on their financial position. The First Anglo-Dutch War (1652–54) began when a Dutch ship refused to salute the English. The war continued for a year after the Rump was dissolved and was finally ended when Cromwell signed the Treaty of Westminster in 1654, hoping to forge an alliance with the Dutch.

! Support or challenge? a

Below is a sample essay-style question which asks how far you agree with a specific statement. Below this is a series of general statements which are relevant to the question. Using your own knowledge and the information on pages 50–52 decide whether these statements support or challenge the statement in the question and tick the appropriate box.

'The threat of Royalism was Cromwell's most important concern during the rule of the Rump, 1649–April 1653.' Assess the validity of this view.

STATEMENT	SUPPORT	CHALLENGE
The Navigation Act and First Anglo-Dutch War		
The Third Civil War		
The Rump's suppression of the Levellers		
The Toleration Act		
Cromwell's massacres at Wexford and Drogheda		
The abolition of the monarchy and House of Lords		
The formation of the Hale Commission to propose legal reforms		
Cromwell's dissolution of the Rump in April 1653		

i Recommended reading

Below is a list of suggested further reading on this topic.

- *The Rump Parliament, 1648–53*, pages 237–65, Blair Worden (2008)
- *The English Republic, 1649–1660*, pages 14–7, T.C Barnard (1997)
- *The Stuart Age, 1603–1714*, pages 242–54, Barry Coward (2011)

i Analysing interpretations a

Study the argument in the extract below and use your contextual knowledge to decide how convincing it is.

Key argument	Evidence that agrees	Evidence that disagrees

EXTRACT A

From Blair Worden, The Rump Parliament 1648–53 *(2008).*

The eclipse of the royalists, and consequently the army's willingness to put pressure on parliament, gave a new volume and intensity to the radical reform movement. Before Worcester [the defeat of Charles II in the Third Civil War], it had been possible to regard the respective demands for moderate and for radical reform as differing only in degree; now it was evident that they differed in kind... The growth of extremist religious views was still more alarming. In the 1640s, battles fought over toleration had been conducted on the familiar territory of biblical quotation and counter-quotation: in the early 1650s radicals, turning against the puritans whose attitudes had been formed in opposition but who were now themselves in power, propounded notions which went against the grain of parliamentary puritanism.

The Rump Parliament, 1649–53

The failure of the radical groups

Although radical groups – such as the Levellers and Diggers – expected religious toleration, they gained very little. A number of Acts regarding religious toleration were passed by the Rump.

- The Toleration Act of 1650 removed the requirement for people to attend church as long as they took part in a religious service each week. Those dissenting groups that did not take part in regular religious services were therefore penalised.

- Nothing was done to remove tithes (church taxes) and in April 1652, the Rump declared that the collection of tithes should continue. Members of radical groups were therefore expected to pay towards the upkeep of a parish church they would never attend.

- The Blasphemy Act of 1650 was aimed at restricting radical religious sects, who could be subject to severe penalties.

- Many of the more eccentric groups were short-lived as a result of the Rump's actions, with the exception of the Quakers. They had spread rapidly in the north in 1650–52 under the leadership of George Fox. Another group, the Baptists, were able to survive because they distanced themselves from the Levellers, with whom they were once associated.

- With the Church courts abolished, some moral offences that they dealt with were now punished in the secular court system. The Adultery Act was passed in May 1650. This imposed the death penalty for adultery, although it was rarely used.

- Censorship of printed material was introduced in order to limit radical pamphlets.

- A government newspaper, *Mercurius Politicus*, was launched to defend the actions of the Rump.

- An Act was passed enforcing the observance of the Sabbath (Sunday) as a holy day, thus excluding groups that did not follow this practice.

- An 'Act for the Propagation of the Gospel in Northern England and Wales' was passed. This controlled the appointment of the clergy so that only approved ministers were allowed to preach.

Successes of the Rump Parliament

- The law that required compulsory attendance at Church was repealed in the Toleration Act, giving a measure of religious freedom.

- An Act ending imprisonment for debt was passed in September 1649.

- The Navigation Act, passed in 1651, stated that goods imported to England and its territories had to be carried on English ships. This was designed to remove the Dutch monopoly on freight trade across northern Europe and North America.

- The army was successful in defeating Royalists in Ireland and Scotland.

- The use of English in legal proceedings, rather than Latin, was authorised.

- The Hale Commission was created in December 1651. Chaired by the senior lawyer Matthew Hale, it was tasked with investigating legal reform.

- The Army was successful in suppressing threats from the Levellers. In particular, a mutiny of Leveller soldiers at Burford in May 1649 resulted in several of their leaders being shot.

Failures of the Rump Parliament

- Despite meeting three times per week for a year, the Hale Commission saw each of its recommendations rejected by the Rump in late 1652.

- Because of the need to maintain a large standing army, there was a shortfall in tax revenue. Without reliable support from the Political Nation, the regime could not reduce or dispense with the Army, but as long as an army existed, that reliable support would not be forthcoming. Despite the Rump resorting to the sale of Crown lands to raise money, the shortfall totalled £700,000 in 1653.

- Many of the greater gentry and nobility refused to co-operate with the regime, leaving a small number of lesser gentry in charge.

- The rate of reform slowed down with time. In 1649, 125 Acts of Parliament were passed, reducing to just 51 in 1652.

- In order to pay for the construction of warships, the monthly assessment was raised to £90,000. The assessment alone now raised as much money as Charles's entire annual revenue.

- As time passed, the Rump appeared more selfish and corrupt. It failed to dissolve itself, despite promises to do so.

Simple essay style

Below is a sample exam question. Use your own knowledge and the information on the opposite page to produce a plan for this question. Choose four general points, and provide three pieces of specific information to support each general point. Once you have planned your essay, write the introduction and conclusion for the essay. The introduction should list the points to be discussed in the essay. The conclusion should summarise the key points and justify which point was the most important.

'Religious divisions meant that the Rump of 1649–53 was always destined to fail.' Assess the validity of this view.

Complete the paragraph

Below are a sample essay-style question and a paragraph written in answer to this question. The paragraph contains a point and a concluding explanatory link back to the question, but lacks examples. Complete the paragraph, adding examples in the space provided.

'Radical religious groups were more of a threat to the Rump Parliament than the Royalists.' Assess the validity of this view.

In many respects, the radical groups were a huge threat to the Rump and this is why they took such harsh measures to restrict their activities.

_____

_____

Thus, the problems posed by the radical groups meant that the Rump could not make sufficient progress in the areas it wanted to reform.

Analysing interpretations

How convincing is Extract A of the achievements of the Rump in the years 1649 to 1653?

Study the arguments in the extract, and use your contextual knowledge to decide how convincing they are. You could shade the sections of the extract that you agree with.

EXTRACT A

From Barry Coward, The Stuart Age _(1980)._

[BT01] The Rump was not a revolutionary regime; was it a competent one? Historical opinion in the past has been fairly unanimous in condemning the Rump as a dilatory, corrupt regime, which subordinated public concerns to the private interests of its members.... Too often modern standards have been used to condemn it. If seen in the context of its own time, the Rump achieved international respectability, and its enemies in the local communities at home were forced into a grudging recognition that republican government was not a recipe for social anarchy, but rather a bulwark against it....

Perhaps the most notable achievement of the Rump was not its glittering foreign and commercial policies, but that, despite high odds against it, it made republican government tolerable to many.

The Parliament of Saints, 1653, and the Instrument of Government

REVISED

The Parliament of Saints

Impact of the Rump

The fact that proposed reforms to the law could not be agreed upon coupled with the necessity to maintain a large standing army meant that the Rump was destined to fail. The army became dissatisfied with the slow pace of reform and eventually Cromwell closed the Rump down by force in April 1653.

Unsure of the next step after dissolving the Rump, Cromwell was advised by the Fifth Monarchist, Major General Harrison, to ask the various churches and radical groups to nominate an assembly of devout men in order to create a godly society. Although short-lived, the Parliament of Saints passed a number of relatively progressive reforms.

Success

- Its members attempted to secure trade routes by continuing the war with the Dutch.
- Legal measures to help debtors were introduced.
- Regulations concerning the treatment of people considered lunatics were introduced.
- Civil marriage was allowed, officiated by JPs.
- The assembly included members form Wales, Scotland and Ireland, making it the first Parliament to represent all of Britain.

Failure

- The commonly used nickname for this Parliament, the 'Barebones Parliament', comes from the name of one of its more radical members, Praise-God Barebone. However, the majority of its members were from the lesser gentry, who were conservative by nature and were not interested in reform.
- The 140 members were not just selected by the Independent Churches, as first suggested. The Council of Officers in the Army added several names, including Cromwell and other senior generals.
- There was a clear split between the radical 'saints' and the conservative members. The propertied members were unhappy at the suggestion that the assembly abolish tithes, which were key to their financial wellbeing.

The Instrument of Government

The Parliament of Saints was assembled in July 1653 and lasted less than six months. On 12 December, the more conservative members met and voted to dissolve the assembly. Major General John Lambert produced the Instrument of Government three days later, offering an entirely new constitution.

- It was modelled on the Heads of the Proposals issued by Ireton in 1647 and served as the constitutional basis of Cromwell's power.
- Executive authority was vested in Cromwell as Lord Protector, with a Council of State of 21 members.
- A single-chamber Parliament acted as the legislative branch of government, with 460 members.
- Parliaments were to be elected every three years by male voters with at least £200 of personal property.
- Cromwell was to remain head of the New Model Army.
- On Cromwell's death, a new protector would be elected by the Council of State.
- There would be a (Presbyterian) state Church, but freedom of worship was granted for all except Catholics.

Simple essay style

Below is a sample exam question. Use your own knowledge and the information on the opposite page to produce a plan for this question. Choose four general points, and provide three pieces of specific information to support each general point. Once you have planned your essay, write the introduction and conclusion for the essay. The introduction should list the points to be discussed in the essay. The conclusion should summarise the key points and justify which point was the most important.

To what extent were religious divisions responsible for the failure of republican governments in the years 1649-53?

 Developing an argument

Below are a sample essay-style question, some key points to be made in the essay and a paragraph from the essay. Read the question, the plan and the sample paragraph. Write the next paragraph on the Parliament of Saints in order to develop the argument further.

'Cromwell desired a godly society more than personal advancement in the years 1649–58.' Assess the validity of this view.

Some key points could include:

- The rule of the Rump Parliament
- The Parliament of Saints

Sample paragraph (Rump Parliament)

The rule of the Rump Parliament in the years 1649–53 is clear evidence that Cromwell desired a more godly and reformed society. A government newspaper was introduced to ensure that the right moral messages were being sent to the public; however, it could also be argued that this censorship of printed material enabled and promoted Cromwell's personal dictatorship. The passing of the Toleration Act in 1650 was ostensibly designed to give religious freedom to dissenting groups. This was also difficult to establish in practice, as dissenters still had to attend some sort of service once a week. The Adultery Act was passed, imposing the death penalty, but it was rarely enforced and again shows a lack of genuinely godly reform.

Next paragraph (Parliament of Saints)

_____

_____

_____

_____

_____

The Protectorate, 1653–59

The First Protectorate Parliament, 1654–55

As Lord Protector, Cromwell wanted to enact a 'reformation of manners' by improving moral behaviour. There were some initial successes for the First Protectorate Parliament.

- Eighty-four ordinances were issued pertaining to moral behaviour and improving local government and infrastructure.
- Bear-baiting and cock-fighting were banned.
- Postal services were improved.
- The maintenance of roads was prioritised.
- Laws were passed to prohibit blasphemy and drunkenness.

Despite some success in the role of Lord Protector, Cromwell faced the same fundamental problems as the Rump. His own concern for the army and the men who served in it appear to have been foremost in his mind. A number of republican MPs who felt excluded from power as a result of his preference for his military associates refused to recognise the Instrument of Government. Cromwell dissolved the Parliament in January 1655.

The Major Generals, 1655–56

Cromwell had always relied on the support of the military in order to maintain himself in power. The last years of the Protectorate were marked by the threat of Royalism and the imposition of military government.

Penruddock's Rising

In the spring of 1655, a Royalist rising led by John Penruddock broke out in Wiltshire and, although it was easily defeated, Cromwell decided it showed that greater control of the provinces was needed.

Military government

Cromwell imposed centralised military rule over the entire country by dividing it into 11 districts, each under the command of a Major General. They would be responsible for local government and security, and were encouraged to attempt a reformation of manners across the social spectrum. The Major Generals were to be assisted in their task by a new militia, to be paid for by a 10 per cent tax on the estates of Royalists.

Reasons for failure

The effectiveness of the government of Major Generals was mixed.

- In Lancashire, Major General Worsley closed down 200 ale houses.
- In Lincolnshire, Major General Whalley suppressed traditional entertainments including stage plays and horse racing.
- Others seem to have neglected many of their duties and did not apply themselves with enthusiasm.
- The replacement of local elites by outsiders imposed by central government was unpopular.
- The low social standing of some of the Major Generals caused resentment from gentry under their control.

The Second Protectorate Parliament, 1656

Elections were held in the summer of 1656. The Council of State excluded 100 known opponents of one-man rule who had sat in the First Protectorate Parliament. This more compliant Parliament passed social reform Acts aimed at improving the efficiency of poor relief and providing more employment.

The Humble Petition and Advice

With the rule of the Major Generals clearly unpopular, Cromwell recognised the need to compromise and accepted the idea of a new constitution. The Humble Petition and Advice was a new constitutional document offered to Cromwell and it consisted of the following:

- Government by a king (changed to Lord Protector when Cromwell refused the Crown).
- The Lords and Commons to govern with the Protector.
- Provision for a hereditary succession.
- Parliament to control the army, and officers of state to be approved by Parliament.
- Regular elections and limited religious toleration. By offering Cromwell the crown, his MPs were attempting to restore a system where the powers and privileges of the leader were established and known, rather than another experimental government.

Why did Cromwell decline the crown?

- He was concerned about how the army would react to him being given the crown by a civilian Parliament.
- A number of commanders in the army made it clear that they would not support Cromwell if he took the crown.
- If he accepted the crown from Parliament, Cromwell would be vesting more power in them than in the army, which had always served to protect his interests.
- He may have been genuinely concerned that accepting the crown was not part of God's plan for him.

a

Spot the mistake

Below are a sample essay-style question and an introductory paragraph written in answer to this question. Why does this paragraph not get into Level 4? Once you have identified the mistake, rewrite the paragraph so that it displays the qualities of Level 4. The mark scheme on page 5 will help you.

'The republic only survived because of the strength of Oliver Cromwell's personality.' Assess the validity of this view.

> Cromwell had a strong personality that meant people listened to him. He had made a name for himself as an inspirational cavalry commander and on several occasions his strong, forceful personality helped him to get his own way politically. This was evident when he decided to rule with the Major Generals.

Recommended reading

Below is a list of suggested further reading on this topic.
- *Cromwell, Our Chief of Men*, pages 694–734, Antonia Fraser (2008)
- *The English Civil Wars, 1640–1660*, pages 103–45, Blair Worden (2010)
- *Oliver Cromwell*, pages 125–141, Barry Coward (2000)

Comparing interpretations

Read the two interpretations below about the character and motivation of Oliver Cromwell. For each, identify the arguments you agree with, listing supporting evidence; and identify the arguments you disagree with, listing supporting evidence.

EXTRACT A

From G M Trevelyan, History of England *(1934).*

The riddle of Oliver must be read not in his mutable opinions but in his constant character. His moderation and his dislike of force were often counteracted by his instinct at every cost to find a practical solution for the problem of the moment. If agreement failed, as it often does in revolutionary times, then, however reluctantly, he would act decisively. Moreover, although commonsense was the dominating quality of his intellect, it worked in an atmosphere of temperamental enthusiasm which left him no doubts or fears when once he had reached a conclusion after weeks of brooding hesitation. For his final resolve, when at last it emerged, always seemed to him the inspiration of God.

EXTRACT B

From Barry Coward, The Stuart Age *(1980).*

How does one harmonize the conflicting facets of Cromwell's undoubtedly ambiguous character?... The correct answer may be, not that Cromwell was a hypocrite or a disillusioned idealist, but that he was someone who oscillated with alarming rapidity from revolutionary enthusiasm to cautious temporizing and vice versa.... At times he appeared to take decisions suddenly, inexplicably, and to be elated with millenarian enthusiasm; at other times he was as tortured by indecision and as careful in building political alliances based on compromise and conciliation as Elizabeth I. Sometimes it is difficult to find reasons for these apparently arbitrary changes of mood.

Charles II and the nature of the restored monarchy

The problem of succession

Cromwell had accepted the need for a clear succession to be established before his death. The Humble Petition had been passed in the context of a number of assassination plots against him, and this made a clear succession an important consideration. As the Instrument of Government had made provisions for an elective succession, it appeared that Major General Lambert would be voted as successor and further military rule was not desired by Parliament.

Shortly before his death in 1658, Cromwell declared that his inexperienced son, Richard, should become Lord Protector, bypassing his more qualified (although younger) son, Henry. Before this, he may have nominated another Major General, Charles Fleetwood, who was married to Cromwell's daughter, Bridget.

Political vacuum after the death of Cromwell

As soon as he succeeded his father, Richard Cromwell summoned the brief Third Protectorate Parliament to meet in January 1659. Richard was a civilian and, unlike his father, he had no experience of warfare. He was unacceptable to the Council of Officers, who forced him to resign later in 1659 and then recalled the Rump. The newly restored Rump appeared to have learned nothing from its earlier failures and the ruling minority began disintegrating rapidly. In October, the army closed it down by force.

Negotiations for the return of the monarchy

General Monck

George Monck was the leader of the Army in Scotland. He was a former Royalist but had worked closely with Cromwell. Fearful that the country was sliding towards military rule, he assembled an army to bring the Rump to power once again.

The return of the Long Parliament

The Army sent a force north under Lambert to counter the threat of Monck but other members of the Army reinstated the Rump once again. Lambert lost support and was sent to the Tower, and Monck entered England in January 1660. Against the wishes of the Rump, Monck moved to reverse Pride's Purge. In March, the restored Long Parliament voted to dissolve itself, leading to elections for the Convention Parliament.

The Convention Parliament and the Restoration

The newly elected Parliament included a number of Royalists and excluded many of the republicans who had been involved in government since Charles's execution. It was accepted that the monarchy should be restored, although Monck had already begun secret negotiations with Charles II. Charles sent his own proposals for a settlement, the Declaration of Breda, and this was accepted by MPs.

Why was Charles restored?

Historians have put forward various arguments to explain why the monarchy was restored in 1660.

- It has been argued that a rejection of the republican governments of the 1650s was inevitable after the return to one-person rule under Cromwell.
- There was fear of another civil war in the context of the political uncertainty of 1659.
- The number of radical religious groups alarmed the Political Nation in the late 1650s. In 1659 there were as many as 60,000 Quakers.
- As the republic had collapsed so quickly, it was essential to men of property that a stable government be restored.
- Charles's Declaration of Breda made him look like an attractive option. He offered religious toleration and payment of arrears to the Army.

Mind map

Use the information on the opposite page to add detail to the mind map below in order to develop your understanding of why the monarchy was restored.

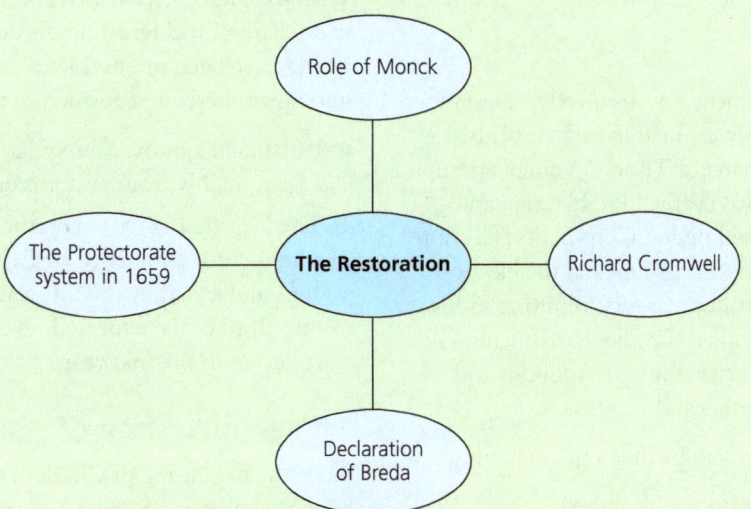

RAG – Rate the timeline   a

Below is a sample exam-style question and a timeline. Read the question, study the timeline and using three coloured pens, put a red, amber or green star next to the events to show:

Red: events and policies that have no relevance to the question

Amber: events and policies that have some significance to the question

Green: events and policies that are directly relevant to the question

'The only successes of the republican governments of 1649–60 were in military affairs.' Assess the validity of this view.

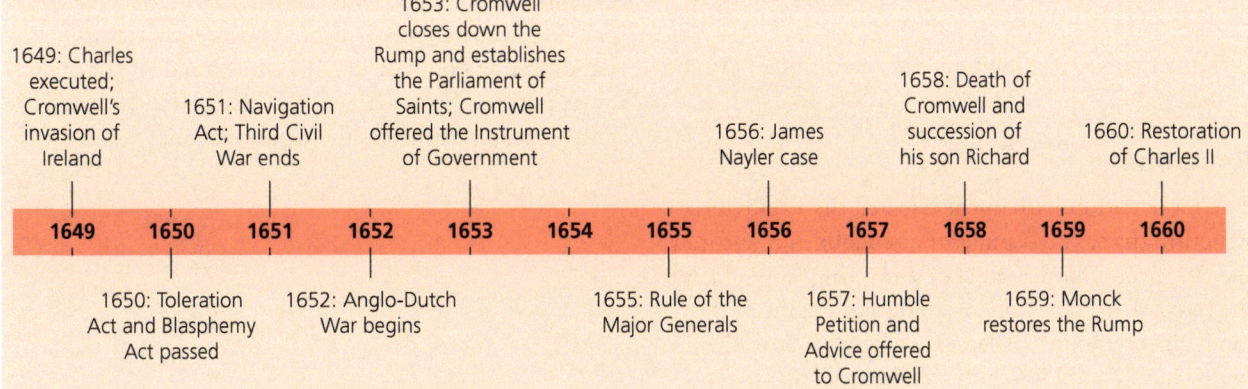

Now repeat the activity with the following question:

To what extent was Oliver Cromwell's government only successful because of the support of the Army?

The emergence of Court and Country 'parties'

The Restoration Settlement, 1660–64

Political

The Convention Parliament was dissolved in December 1660 and new elections were held in early 1661. In London, the Fifth Monarchist Thomas Venner attempted an uprising and there was nearly a Presbyterian and Independent coup in the London Corporation elections. This reignited fears of radical groups and the elections produced a massive Royalist majority, resulting in the appointment of the so-called Cavalier Parliament. The new Parliament was overwhelmingly Anglican and suspicious of both Catholics and dissenters.

The new political settlement included the following:

- The prerogative courts were abolished.
- The 1641 Triennial Act was renewed but crucially did not include any mechanisms to enforce the calling of a Parliament every three years. This meant that Charles would be able to resort to personal rule if he desired.
- Parliament ensured that they controlled the militia, although the Militia Act of 1661 stated that the king alone was in supreme overall command of the armed forces.
- The Privy Council remained the most important organ of government and Charles doubled its size to 120 in order to accommodate an increasing number of different factions. This made it difficult to manage, so Charles relied on a small inner circle, headed by Edward Hyde, Earl of Clarendon.
- The Licensing Act reintroduced censorship of printed material.

Religious

The Convention Parliament rejected the Presbyterian structure that existed under the republic and restored the Anglican Church. In 1661 a meeting was held at the Savoy Palace in London to discuss details of the long-term religious settlement. Although both the high-church and low-church factions were represented, the impact of Venner's rising and the election of the Cavalier Parliament meant that High Anglicanism would now dominate. The four Acts of the Clarendon Code (discussed on page 62) reflected the nature of this settlement.

Financial

With the prerogative courts abolished, many of the taxes that Charles I had relied upon (such as Ship Money) would have been impossible to enforce. The financial settlement therefore consisted of the following.

- Parliament approved a regular income of £1.2 million a year, mainly from customs duties and excise taxes.
- The Hearth Tax (based on the number of fireplaces in a house) was authorised by Parliament in November 1661 and levied in 1662. It was disappointing as only one-third of the expected revenue of £250,000 was collected in the first year.

The emergence of parties

Since the beginning of Charles I's reign, a division had begun to emerge between 'Court' and 'Country' interests. Members of the Political Nation – particularly in Parliament – who were suspicious of Charles's links to Catholic powers and the Arminians formed the Country faction against Court interests.

The two factions became more defined from the early 1670s. The Country faction believed that Charles II's pro-French policies were damaging to the nation, and his attempts to provide toleration to both Catholics and dissenters were dangerous.

Charles's group of pro-Catholic advisers, known as the Cabal (discussed on page 66) suffered a decline in the early 1670s and Thomas Osborne, Earl of Danby, became Treasurer and chief adviser. His views were pro-Anglican and pro-Dutch. He concentrated on building a support base of MPs who would be prepared to support the Crown now it had changed direction. This group became known as the Court faction.

Interpretation: content or argument? **a**

Read the following interpretation on the character of Charles II and the two alternative answers to the question. Which answer focuses more on the content and which focuses more on the arguments of the interpretation? Explain your answer.

With reference to your understanding of the historical context, assess how convincing the arguments in this extract are in relation to the character of Charles II.

Answer 1

The extract shows that when Charles spent time in exile he was able to interact with ordinary people and 'knew what it was like to be a commoner'. He also acted in a distinguished and dignified way when he was living at the French court.

Answer 2

The underlying point made in the extract is that Charles was different to other monarchs. It is heavily implied that the experiences he went through during exile were generally positive and prepared him well for kingship. However, because he lacked finance in these years he was unable to fulfil his potential.

EXTRACT A

From B. Weiser, Charles II and the Politics of Access *(2003).*

Unlike any other monarchs of his age, Charles II's experiences before he gained the throne gave him a unique insight into the dynamics of access. While other monarchs (for instance, his great-grandfather James V) may have masqueraded themselves for a few hours or days, Charles knew what it was like to be a commoner. During the six weeks that Charles II spent disguised as a common servant to escape Cromwell's army, he was able to interact with his subjects as their peer. In his exile, heads of state recognised his dignity in ceremonies, but he lacked the financial resources to maintain the trappings of majesty.

Develop the detail

Below are a sample essay-style question and a paragraph written in answer to this question. The paragraph contains a limited amount of detail. Annotate the paragraph to add additional detail to the answer.

'The inadequate Restoration settlement meant that Charles II was always going to face instability.' Assess the validity of this view.

The Restoration settlement clarified a number of the powers of the monarch but also left a lot of questions unanswered. The Triennial Act was revised, which in theory meant that a Parliament was to be called every three years, however, there was no mechanism to enforce this. The financial settlement was also weak, as Charles was unable to raise adequate revenue.

The restoration of the Church of England

The Clarendon Code

As the Cavalier Parliament was overwhelmingly Anglican, its members moved to restore the Church of England to its former status. Between 1661 and 1665, four Acts were passed that became known as the Clarendon Code.

- The Corporation Act of 1661 restricted non-Anglicans from sitting on borough corporations.
- The Act of Uniformity of 1662 stated that parish priests should once again accept the Book of Common Prayer. One thousand eight hundred ministers were unable to conform and were expelled and deprived of their livings.
- The Conventicle Act of 1664 restricted dissenters from meeting in groups outside the Church of England.
- The Five Mile Act forbade ministers expelled under the Act of Uniformity from going within five miles of their former parishes.

Charles's attempts to establish toleration and Parliament's resistance

First Declaration of Indulgence

In 1662, Charles attempted to suspend the Act of Uniformity and issued a Declaration of Indulgence, which would have allowed for both dissenters and Catholics to worship with relative freedom. This was resisted by a combination of bishops in the House of Lords and MPs.

The Second Anglo-Dutch War and the Treaty of Dover

Charles's pro-French foreign policy saw England fight the Second Anglo-Dutch War between 1665 and 1667. This ended in disaster when the Dutch were able to break the chain that blocked the Medway River in June 1667 and destroy 13 English ships at anchor on the other side. Charles signed the Treaty of Dover with the French in 1670, committing England to a further war with the Dutch. At the time the public were unaware of a secret clause that necessitated Charles to announce his own conversion to Catholicism at an appropriate time, in exchange for French subsidies that would free Charles from dependence on Parliaments. A second pact with Louis XIV in 1675 committed more money to Charles, with the first payment of £100,000 being made in 1681, enabling Charles to embark on personal rule for the last four years of his reign.

Second Declaration of Indulgence and the Test Act

In 1672, with Parliament not in session, Charles issued another Declaration of Indulgence. As long as Parliament was not sitting the Indulgence could be maintained, but Charles was facing major financial problems and had to suspend payments to his creditors in what became known as the Stop of the Exchequer. Obliged by the Treaty of Dover to join the Third Anglo-Dutch War (1672–74), Charles had little choice but to turn to Parliament for funds. In exchange, MPs insisted on the passing of a Test Act in place of the Indulgence, which forced holders of public office to deny key Catholic doctrines.

Conclusion

The dominance of the Church of England was thus ensured once again, and the most high-profile victims of the Test Act were Lord Treasurer Clifford and Charles's Catholic brother, James, who was Lord Admiral. The Church of England had been restored, but the old problems of maintaining religious stability in the face of both the Catholic and dissenting threat had not gone away.

Mind map

Use the information on the opposite page to add detail to the mind map below.

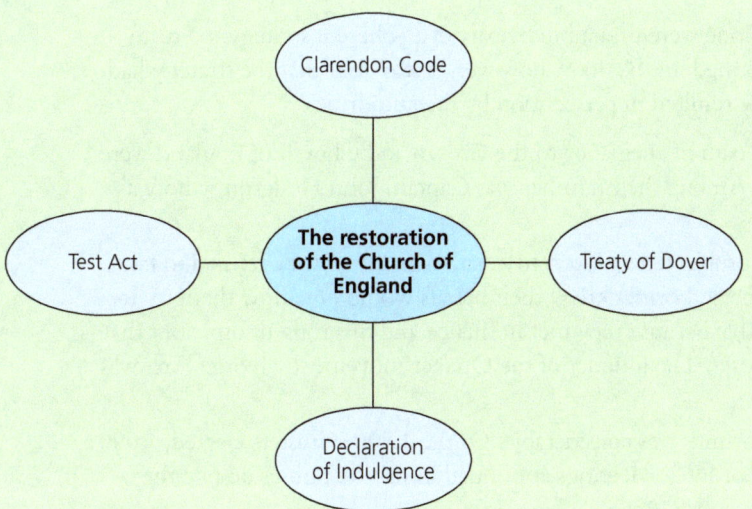

Clarendon Code

Test Act

The restoration of the Church of England

Treaty of Dover

Declaration of Indulgence

 Eliminate irrelevance **a**

Below are a sample A-level exam question and a paragraph written in answer to this question. Read the paragraph and identify parts of the paragraph that are not directly relevant to the question. Draw a line through the information that is irrelevant and justify your deletions in the margin.

'Religious issues were central to the discontent faced by governments in the years 1649–1672.' Assess the validity of this view.

Religious issues made relations with Parliament and governing the country effectively a very difficult task. There was a fundamental disagreement between Charles II and Parliament over the future of the Church of England. Charles wanted to secure toleration for both dissenters and Catholics and attempted to issue two Declarations of Indulgence in 1662 and 1672. As well as this, the Triennial Act was passed in 1664. This was the same as the original Act of 1641 but failed to include any mechanisms to enforce the calling of a Parliament at least once every three years.

Charles II and dissenters

Persecution

The four Acts of the Clarendon Code were undoubtedly part of a coherent strategy to create uniformity of worship across the kingdom. By 1669, however, it was clear that the strategy had failed. Continued non-conformity resulted in persecution by the authorities.

● Those who refused to take the oath of allegiance to the Crown and Church of England were arrested and often imprisoned. Among their number was Captain John Hodgson, who was arrested five times in 18 months.

● Passed in 1662, the Quaker Act subjected Quakers to severe penalties if they refused to take the oath of allegiance, which the authorities knew their beliefs would not allow them to do. They were particularly vulnerable because they met in silence and this roused suspicions that they met for other, secret purposes. The founder of the Quaker movement, George Fox, was arrested in 1664.

● The impact of the Act of Uniformity was considerable. Of the 1,800 ministers ejected, 1,000 left the Church in the summer of 1662. Meetings continued in private houses despite the danger of arrest under the Conventicle Act.

● The Corporation Act ensured that the influence of dissenters was vastly reduced on borough corporations.

● A second Conventicle Act was passed in 1670, which was harsher than the first Act.

Successes for dissenters

● Some dissenting ministers benefited from association with wealthy merchants or landowners, and were offered payments for preaching. The main beneficiaries of this generosity were the Presbyterians, with a group founded by John Canne receiving £20 a year from Lady Dorothy Norcliffe.

● There was little popular enthusiasm for the Clarendon Code, and the Acts were not enforced consistently or effectively.

● In 1667, the first Conventicle Act expired, which led to a flurry of activity by dissenters. In 1669, a Presbyterian academy was founded and meeting houses were beginning to be built again. Further training academies were later built, and ministers' associations formed in the early 1670s.

● When Charles issued the Declaration of Indulgence in 1672, he was suspending the laws that persecuted dissenters and proposing that they be allowed the freedom not to attend church and meet in licensed gatherings of their own. A number of licences were given to dissenting congregations and although the Indulgence was withdrawn in 1673, the licences were not recalled until 1675.

● In 1676, when Danby carried out a census of dissenting groups in a bid to persuade Charles that persecution should be renewed, it was only partially completed and failed in its main purpose.

Why did dissenters survive the years of persecution?

● Those who left the Church, both voluntarily and because of ejection, were generally committed to their principles.

● The dissenters received sympathy from many, and the authorities were often half-hearted in their attempts to impose persecuting laws.

● As uniformity was defined on a narrow basis (accepting the Book of Common Prayer being the main criteria), the number of people classified as dissenters increased and they were therefore not isolated.

Simple essay style

Below is a sample exam question. Use your own knowledge and the information on the opposite page to produce a plan for this question. Choose four general points, and provide three pieces of specific information to support each general point. Once you have planned your essay, write the introduction and conclusion for the essay. The introduction should list the points to be discussed in the essay. The conclusion should summarise the key points and justify which point was the most important.

'The Cavalier Parliament were successful in restoring the authority of the Church of England in the years 1660 to 1678.' Assess the validity of this view.

 ## Spectrum of importance

Below are a sample essay-style question and a list of events and situations that could be referred to when answering the question. Use your own knowledge and the information in this section to reach a judgement about the importance of these general points to the question posed. Write numbers on the spectrum below to indicate their relative importance. Having done this, write a brief justification of your placement, explaining why some of these factors are more important than others. The resulting diagram could form the basis of an essay plan.

How accurate is it to describe Charles II as sympathetic to dissenters in the years 1660–78?

1 The oath of allegiance to Crown and Church of England

2 The Declaration of Indulgence, 1672

3 Danby's failed census of dissenters

4 The Second Conventicle Act

5 The Act of Uniformity

Least important ←——————————————————→ Most important

Catholic influence at Court

Catholic influence in England

The Cabal

After the Restoration there were signs of a renewed concern with the threat of Catholic influence. In 1666, the Great Fire of London sparked rumours of Catholic agents at work, and the spread of plague led Charles to allow Parliament to blame his chief adviser, Clarendon, who was replaced in 1667 with a group known as the Cabal. The group took its name from the names of the five ministers involved (**C**lifford, **A**rlington, **B**uckingham, **A**shley and **L**auderdale). Two of its members, Clifford and Arlington, were Catholics.

The impact of James's conversion

In 1668, Charles's brother, the Duke of York, converted to Catholicism, a fact that became public knowledge by 1669. James's conversion was made plain when he refused to take Anglican Communion, and when he resigned the office of Lord Admiral his conversion was in no doubt. The prospect of a Catholic heir was in the forefront of MPs minds and the Whig faction would later work to remove him from the succession.

Conflicts with Parliament over Catholicism

The announcement of the Declaration of Indulgence in 1672 explicitly permitted Catholics to worship in private. This produced hostile reactions in Parliament for two reasons.

- The Catholic sympathies of Charles and his brother had become increasingly apparent.
- Apart from the religious issue, Parliament was just as concerned with Charles's apparent willingness to dispense with the law. This action echoed that of continental Catholic monarchs.

After 1672, fear of both Catholicism and absolutism increased markedly, as Charles was seen to be attempting to emulate Louis XIV in what was now an unapologetic way. While James's daughter Mary was married to a Protestant, William of Orange, from 1677 (in a marriage arranged by Danby), James himself was permitted to wed the Catholic Mary of Modena. As Charles had no legitimate children, the likelihood that James would succeed his brother increased.

Charles II and continental Catholicism

In 1667, Louis XIV invaded the Spanish Netherlands and attacked the Dutch. This fed an awareness in England that Catholic France was the biggest threat the country faced. Outwardly, English diplomats negotiated a Triple Alliance with Protestant Sweden and the United Provinces, but at the same time Charles was making early arrangements for the Treaty of Dover through his sister Henrietta, who was married to the French king's brother. Charles favoured this pro-French policy for a number of reasons.

- His mother was French and he had spent time at the French court during his exile.
- His sister Henrietta, who married into the French royal family, was his favourite sibling.
- He looked to France as an example to follow in the fields of art, culture and philosophy.

Relations with Louis XIV

As well as the Treaty of Dover in 1670 and the subsequent agreement in 1675 that Louis would fund Charles if necessary, another secret arrangement was made in 1677. This time, Louis offered even more money and it was backed by a further treaty in 1678 in which Charles agreed to disband his army of 30,000 men in return for further funds.

Analysing interpretations

Using your understanding of the historical context, assess how convincing the arguments in these three extracts are in relation to Charles II's attitude to Catholicism.

Study the arguments in the three extracts, and use your contextual knowledge to decide how convincing they are.

You could shade the sections of each extract that you agree with.

Then set out the plan of answer identifying convincing arguments and unconvincing arguments, using your contextual knowledge.

Extract	Arguments you find convincing	Supporting evidence	Arguments you do not find convincing	Supporting evidence
A				
B				
C				

EXTRACT A

From W. Young, International Politics and Warfare in the Age of Louis XIV and Peter the Great *(2004).*

He [Charles] planned to accept French subsidies, commercial advantages, and security against Louis XIV in exchange for an offensive alliance against the United Provinces he knew would never take place... After the Treaty of Dover Louis XIV pressured the English monarch to gradually accept the possibility of a Dutch war without the declaration of Catholicism... Charles II had a permanent orientation towards France. This resulted from his family relationship with Louis XIV, admiration for French power and influence in Europe, and his envy of the French monarchy's power in France.

EXTRACT B

From P. Allitt, Catholic Converts: British and American Intellectuals Turn to Rome *(2011).*

Charles II... was closely allied to Louis XIV of France and sympathised with Catholicism but was shrewd enough to disguise his sympathies from a rabidly anti-Catholic population. It remained an act of high treason to convert an English man or woman to Catholicism, and any priest entering England or any Englishman sheltering a priest was liable to capital punishment. The laws were not stringently enforced, but they acted as a permanent deterrent to potential converts... 'Popery' remained bitterly unpopular, and wild fears of a popish plot to blow up the banks of the River Thames, flood the city of London, and kill the King, led to a renewed wave of executions and imprisonments.

EXTRACT C

From A. Fraser, Charles II *(2002).*

He trod delicately to preserve the image of his own personal Protestantism; otherwise, he would not only be restored by the agency of an alien Catholic power, but in the guise of a Catholic alien himself. This is not to exclude visits to Catholic churches and chapels, and even attendance at mass... James Duke of York, who bore less responsibility, leant towards Rome sooner than his brother. The incidence of his visits to Catholic churches may also have increased the stories about the King, since it was easy for rumour to mistake one brother for another.

Exam focus (A-level)

Below is a sample high level answer to an A-level style question. Read it and the comments around it.

'Governments in the years 1649–72 faced instability because Parliaments were unwilling to support radical change.' Assess the validity of this view.

In the years 1649–72, England experienced its only period of republican rule and then reverted back to the Stuart monarchy when it was clear that republican rule was not providing stability. A succession of governments tried and failed to find political stability, and throughout these years there was conflict between members of the Political Nation who were naturally conservative and radicals who wanted to enact reforms. However, other reasons for the failure of republican government include financial problems – partly related to the impact of the military in political affairs – and the impact of religious differences, including the threat of Catholicism.

One of the main reasons why the Rump Parliament (1649–53) failed to act as an effective government was the conservative nature of its membership. As members of the gentry, they felt threatened by radical groups and moved to arrest John Lilburne, the Leveller leader, and his supporters. They also passed the Blasphemy Act, effectively outlawing the more extreme groups such as the Ranters. The fact that limited legal reform was enacted also shows the conservative nature of the regime, and the recommendations of the Hale Commission were rejected in 1652, which was seen as a wasted opportunity by radicals. Both the Rump and Barebones Parliaments failed to abolish tithes as many members of the gentry benefited from them. The Barebones Parliament also faced a split between moderates and radicals, with the moderates eventually persuading Cromwell to close the assembly down by force in 1653. The conservative nature of the Protectorate is shown in the fact that a £200 property qualification was required to vote. Also, in 1657 the Crown was offered to Cromwell, demonstrating that the MPs desired a traditional form of government with a leader having the same constraints as previous monarchs. Overall, by far the most radical action of the republicans was the execution of the king himself. However, this can be seen as a necessity rather than anything based on the ideological convictions of the men who carried it out.

Under the Restored monarchy, too, there was no desire to support radical change. Venner's Fifth Monarchist rising in 1661 spread fear throughout the Political Nation and the pro-Royalist Cavalier Parliament was elected. Their conservatism is evident in the fact that they supported the Clarendon Code. The four Acts of the Clarendon Code were designed to clamp down on dissenting ministers and their congregations, and Acts such as the Conventicle Act – which restricted dissenters from meeting in groups – alienated many. The Quaker Act persecuted Quakers and many were arrested, including their leader George Fox in 1664. All of this was contrary to what Charles II wanted, as he tried to introduce Declarations of Indulgence in 1662 and 1672.

There were a number of financial problems in the period that caused instability. The military became involved in politics on a number of occasions under the republic and this caused financial strain. The New Model Army propped up the Rump Parliament, and it was necessary to levy high taxes in order to maintain a large standing army. There was a shortfall in revenue of £700,000 in 1653 due to the need to fight wars against Royalists in Scotland and Ireland, as well as the Anglo-Dutch War. The amount

The introduction is strong. It focuses clearly on the question, of which it shows an excellent understanding and possible factors are established.

This paragraph directly addresses the factor given in the question with excellent deployment of evidence.

This paragraph develops the argument in favour of the conservative nature of Parliament, although it could be improved by including a summary statement linking it back to the question.

demanded in the assessment tax went up to £90,000 a month. After the Restoration financial issues meant that Charles II and Parliament regularly came to blows. Excise taxes raised £1.2 million, which was still not adequate to cover all costs, so the Hearth Tax was created. This only raised one-third of expected revenue, which meant that Charles eventually had to resort to calling Parliament, who in turn forced him to abandon the Declaration of Indulgence in 1673. Overall, it is clear that financial issues were damaging for both governments, but for quite different reasons. The republic faced financial difficulties partly because of the conservative nature of Parliament. Its members wanted to maintain themselves in power and thus needed a large army that created debts. The Restoration monarchy wanted to fund a pro-French foreign policy and this resulted in its financial problems.

Finally, religious differences meant that government stability was never possible for long. From the very beginning, the Rump aimed to clamp down on religious radicals and the Leveller leaders were arrested in 1649. The Toleration Act was passed in 1650 but there remained a requirement to attend a service every week. During the rule of the Major Generals and the Protectorate, Cromwell attempted to enact a 'reformation of manners', but this was implemented with mixed effectiveness and it is clear that radical religious groups were still a threat after the Restoration because of the impact of Venner's Rising in 1661. This caused a renewed fear of groups such as the Fifth Monarchists and the Cavalier Parliament was elected. This links to Parliament's reluctance to support radical change as this Parliament passed the Clarendon Code and Quaker Act, clamping down on religious dissent. Attempted Declarations of Indulgence in 1662 and 1672 were met with hostility from this largely Anglican Parliament. It is clear, therefore, that religious differences are vital in understanding instability, but they were made worse by the unwillingness of Parliament to embrace radical change.

In conclusion, as long as the members of Parliament and those controlling the regime in the 1650s were conservative and unwilling to embrace change, the interests of the radicals would never be satisfied and therefore the republic was destined to fail. The Restored Parliament was similarly conservative, and the majority of those that sat in Parliament in these years were from traditional gentry families who had always felt they had a right to hold high office.

An impressive paragraph which is very much geared to the question. There is an impressive link between the factor of finances and the previous factor of conservatism.

This paragraph is well explained, relevant and makes links to the previous issue of conservatism in Parliament.

The conclusion weighs the relative significance of the evidence, and reaches a conclusion which reflects the balance of the essay – that as long as those in charge were conservative gentry, the regime could not be entirely successful. The essay concludes as it began. It shows sustained analysis and a comprehensive grasp of the topic.

Level 5 answers are thorough and detailed. They clearly engage with the question and offer a balanced and carefully reasoned argument, which is sustained throughout the essay. This essay meets all the criteria for a Level 5 answer.

Consolidation

This is a long and detailed essay. Without losing the overall argument of the essay, experiment with reducing its length by 100 words. This is a particularly useful exercise for trying to produce an essay which gets to the heart of the question without being over-long.

4 The establishment of a constitutional monarchy, 1678–1702

The Exclusion Crisis, 1678–81

The Popish Plot

In 1678, an Anglican priest named Titus Oates approached the London magistrate Sir Edmund Berry Godfrey with a story of a plot organised by the Jesuits and French to murder Charles II and replace him with his Catholic brother, James. Oates had been educated at a Jesuit school in France, and his story lacked credibility. Shortly afterwards, Godfrey was found dead in a London park and the plot began to be believed.

Investigations revealed that one of those accused by Oates, Edward Coleman, had been in correspondence with Catholics in France. As many of the public now believed his story, Oates was able to accuse anyone he liked for the next year and 35 Catholics were killed in the ensuing hysteria.

The fall of Danby

Those who were suspicious of Charles's growing absolutism, such as the Earl of Shaftesbury, were now able to challenge Danby's power and influence. Impeachment proceedings began against Danby as evidence emerged that he had been accepting French subsidies, and he was sent to the Tower of London where he remained until 1684. Charles dissolved the Cavalier Parliament in 1679 to avoid an escalation of the crisis and new elections produced an anti-Danby majority. These MPs were now known as Whigs.

The Exclusion Bill

The next step was a bill to exclude James from the throne and replace him with Charles's illegitimate Protestant son, James Scott, the Duke of Monmouth. This was a step too far for Charles and he attempted to avoid what he saw as an attack on hereditary Divine Right.

- He dissolved Parliament in 1679 so the Exclusion Bill could not be read by the Lords.
- Another Exclusion Bill was presented in 1680, and this was defeated by the Lords, who were under pressure from Charles as a result of his personal appearances at debates.

Why did Charles survive the Exclusion Crisis?

- Because Charles saw the Exclusion Bill as a direct attack on hereditary Divine Right monarchy, he showed a determination and resolve that contrasted with his apathy in many other matters.
- Charles was able to use his prerogative powers to override Parliament, especially his ability to delay legislation and dissolve Parliament.
- The longer the crisis continued, the fewer MPs were prepared to commit their wholehearted support to the Whig cause. This was because it seemed that the Catholic threat was subsiding.
- Because the first payment of £100,000 from Louis XIV reached Charles in 1681, he was financially independent and was able to work without the need to consult Parliament. He decreed that the 1681 Parliament should meet at Oxford rather than Westminster in order to avoid conflict. When the Whigs passed another Exclusion Bill, he was able to dissolve Parliament and order the arrest of Shaftesbury without concerning himself with the financial consequences.
- As well as arresting Whig leaders in Parliament, Charles purged Whigs from local government, particularly in London and the south-east.

Quick quizzes at www.hoddereducation.co.uk/myrevisionnotes

Support or challenge? **a**

Below is a sample A-level exam style question which asks how far you agree with a specific statement. Below this is a series of events which are relevant to the question. Using your own knowledge and the information on the opposite page decide whether these events support or challenge the statement in the question and tick the appropriate box.

'The Exclusion Crisis was the most important turning point in declining relations between Crown and Parliament, 1660–85.' Assess the validity of this view.

STATEMENT	SUPPORT	CHALLENGE
The Popish Plot		
£100,000 from Louis XIV reaches Charles, 1681		
The Declaration of Indulgence, 1672		
Inadequate revenue raised through the Hearth tax, 1662		
Arrest of Shaftesbury, 1681		
The Test Act, 1673		

i **Developing an argument**

Below are a sample A-level exam-style question, a list of key points to be made in the essay and a paragraph from the essay. Read the question, the plan and the sample paragraph. Rewrite the paragraph in order to develop an argument. Your paragraph should explain why the factor discussed in the paragraph is either the most significant factor or less significant than another factor.

'The monarchy faced more successes than failures in the years 1660–81.' Assess the validity of this view.

Key points

- The Exclusion Crisis
- Financial issues
- Religious issues
- Conflicts with Parliament

Sample paragraph

The Exclusion Crisis was ultimately a success for the monarchy because Charles was able to clamp down on Whig opposition. Parliament attempted to pass three Exclusion Bills between 1679 and 1681 and through personal appearances in the Lords, financial help from Louis XIV and the use of his prerogative powers to close down Parliament, Charles was able to ensure that his brother would follow him as monarch.

The last years of Charles's reign, 1681–85

Persecution of the Whigs

Charles was able to tarnish the reputation of his Whig opponents by presenting them as republicans committed to a violent overthrow of the monarchy similar to that seen in 1649. He was able to bring down Whig opposition in a number of ways in the years 1681–85.

- By using his prerogative powers to control the judiciary, Charles was able to remove a number of leading Whigs from office.
- Several Whigs were executed but Shaftesbury avoided this fate and fled abroad.
- Charles's financial position improved after the Exclusion Crisis, and the Crown was able to raise a total revenue of £1.4 million in 1684–85. Existing excise taxes were utilised but the real cause of financial success was the increased revenue collected via customs duties from improved international trade.
- The Tory faction ensured that the Clarendon Code was enforced with renewed enthusiasm against dissenters.
- Freedom of speech was suppressed and when Whig views were put forward in print the authors were often subject to libel proceedings.

Absolutism and local government

Whigs were removed from local office and this enabled Charles to maintain his personal rule.

- JPs who had previously persecuted Catholics were replaced with men prepared to persecute dissenters.
- Judges who were disloyal lost their jobs. A list was found among Shaftesbury's papers of men in the localities who could sit as judges and be trusted to remain loyal to the Whig cause. Charles's advisers worked through the list and expelled them.
- Two Tory sheriffs were elected in London in 1682, in a contest marred by fraud and violence.
- Charles challenged the borough charters given to a number of towns. These charters gave the towns certain rights and privileges over justice and administration, but Charles revised them and put control of towns in the hands of his own nominees.
- The corporation of the City of London was now controlled by those loyal to the king, and when petitions demanding the exclusion of James were presented to the corporation they were thrown out.

The Rye House Plot

In 1683, a group of old Cromwellian soldiers concocted a plot to kill Charles and replace him with Monmouth. The plot failed and the conspirators were arrested, but it gave Charles the excuse to destroy the remaining Whig leaders. Lord William Russell, Algernon Sidney and Sir Thomas Armstrong were beheaded for their role in the plot. Charles was now able to avoid calling a Parliament for the rest of his reign.

Final years, 1683–85

For the last two years of his life, Charles was content to leave the administration to his brother James and his ministers. The Court felt that if Parliament was restored, it would lead to a war with France and calls to hold new elections were ignored.

Simple essay style

Below is a sample A-level exam question. Use your own knowledge and the information on the opposite page to produce a plan for this question. Choose four general points, and provide three pieces of specific information to support each general point. Once you have planned your essay, write the introduction and conclusion for the essay. The introduction should list the points to be discussed in the essay. The conclusion should summarise the key points and justify which point was the most important.

'Charles II's rule was stable in all areas of policy apart from religion.' Assess the validity of this view.

How far do you agree?

Read the extract below. Using the table, summarise each of its arguments. Use your knowledge to agree or contradict.

Arguments in extract	Knowledge that corroborates	Knowledge that contradicts
1		
2		
3		

EXTRACT A

From R. Ashcraft, Revolutionary Politics and Locke's "Two Treatises of Government" *(1986).*

The discovery of the Rye House Plot and the confessions of several of its participants provided the government with the political leverage it needed to crush the Whig opposition. As James expressed it in a letter to William of Orange, "if the right use be made of this conspiracy... that which was designed to be the destruction of [the monarchy] will prove of great advantage to it." Whatever ambivalent feelings Charles might have had concerning the punishment to be meted out to the conspirators as consequence of Monmouth's participation in the undertaking, James showed little hesitation in taking advantage of the situation to remove his enemies from the political arena. He had always viewed Whigs as closet Republicans, and the Rye House Plot only confirmed his longstanding belief that it was simply the weakness and irresolution of the English monarchy that permitted individuals the freedom of action they enjoyed... James was determined to make every effort to transform the prosecution of the Rye House conspiracy into a justification for absolute monarchy.

4 The establishment of a constitutional monarchy, 1678–1702

The reign of James II, 1685–88

The Monmouth Rebellion

Charles died in 1685 and Monmouth soon raised a rebellion in the West Country. He had been in self-imposed exile in Holland and landed at Lyme Regis in June. The rebellion received little support and Monmouth's followers were subject to harsh punishments. Monmouth himself was executed on his uncle's orders in July. A series of trials known as the 'The Bloody Assizes' began in August and resulted in the executions of hundreds of suspected conspirators.

James and Parliament

Finance

The Parliament that assembled in May 1685 was dominated by Tories supportive of James, primarily because of continued royal interference in the awarding of borough charters. This Parliament was generous in its financial settlement and voted £2 million per year to James, giving him a high degree of independence.

Religion

Later in 1685, James issued personal dispensations to allow Catholics to become army officers and announced that he intended to suspend the Test Acts. Both Whigs and Tories became resistant and voted to restrict James's funding. James adjourned Parliament in November and eventually dissolved it. Fear began to spread among both Tories and Whigs that without Parliament James would attempt to promote Catholicism through his prerogative powers.

When the Scottish Parliament assembled in 1685, James announced that he intended to introduce penal laws against rebellious Presbyterians while advocating toleration for Catholics.

Godden v. Hales

In 1686, Sir Edward Hales, a Catholic, was sued by his coachman, Arthur Godden, for holding a military command without taking Anglican Communion. At the trial it was judged that only the king could decide whether Hales was at fault and whether officers should take the Test Act. This had significant implications because it means that James had legal backing to suspend laws against Catholics.

James and religious toleration

The case of *Godden v. Hales* started a chain of events that would bring James's sympathy for the Catholic Church into sharp focus.

- Some of the highest offices in the land were given to Catholics, and James controversially received the papal ambassador.
- In April 1687, James used the ruling in the *Godden v. Hales* case to issue a Declaration of Indulgence, which would have granted toleration to both dissenters and Catholics.
- James's ultimate aspiration was to convert England to Catholicism and the Indulgence was seen as the first step towards this.
- By issuing the Indulgence, James was also attempting to gain the support of Protestant dissenters as they would be given toleration. A group of administrators was appointed to purge borough corporations of anyone unwilling to accept the Indulgence.
- Catholics were appointed as magistrates and James expelled the Fellows of Magdalen College, Oxford, and replaced them with Catholics.

RAG – Rate the timeline

Below is a sample A-level exam-style question and a timeline. Read the question, study the timeline and using three coloured pens, put a red, amber or green star next to the events to show:

Red: events and policies that have no relevance to the question

Amber: events and policies that have some significance to the question

Green: events and policies that are directly relevant to the question

'Financial issues meant that the governments of Charles II and James II were destined to fail in the years 1660–88.' Assess the validity of this view.

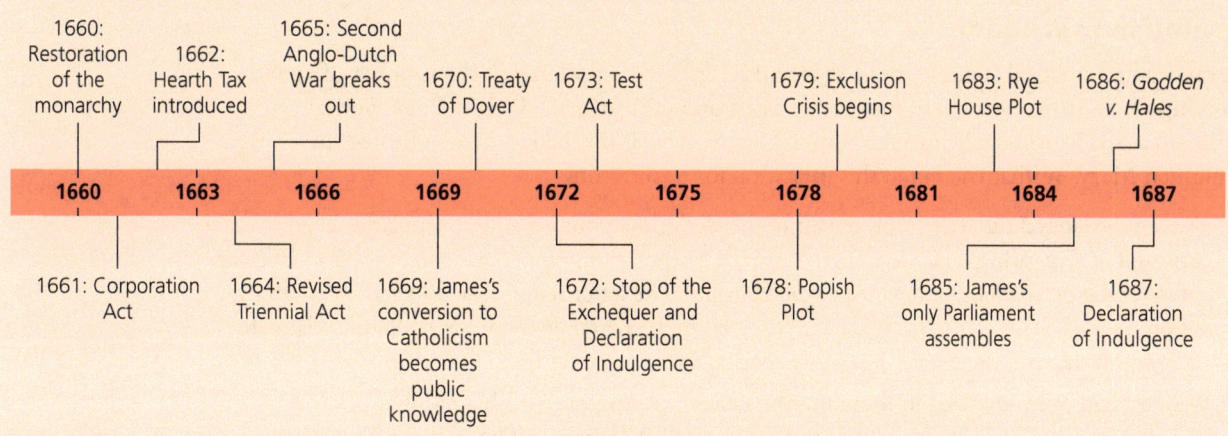

Developing an argument

Below are a sample A-level exam-style question, a list of key points to be made in the essay and a paragraph from the essay. Read the question, the plan and the sample paragraph. This supports the view put forward in the question. Rewrite the paragraph, using a similar number of words, putting forward a counter-argument. Your paragraph should explain why the situation may have been different from that put forward in the sample paragraph. When you have completed your writing, read both paragraphs. Is one or the other more convincing? Or does the truth – in your view – lie somewhere between the two claims?

'Charles II's and James II's sympathy for Catholicism was the main reason for disagreement between Crown and Parliament in 1665–88.' Assess the validity of this view.

Key points
- Sympathy with Catholicism
- Financial issues
- Foreign policy

Sample paragraph

Both Charles and James showed clear sympathy for the Catholic Church. Charles probably converted on his deathbed but during his life he married a Catholic and forged a close alliance with the leading Catholic power, France. In the Treaty of Dover Charles promised to convert and he issued a Declaration of Indulgence in 1672, which would have suspended penal laws against Catholics. James, too, showed that he not only sympathised but wanted England to become a Catholic country again. He converted in the late 1660s and when he became king in 1685, he gave dispensations to allow Catholic army officers to avoid punishment. His Declarations of Indulgence in 1687 and 1688 were part of a wider plan to allow full toleration, which even the Tories in Parliament began to resist. Overall, sympathy with Catholicism is vital in understanding the instability of the period because only a tiny proportion of the population were of the faith and the majority of the Political Nation would never agree to toleration proposals.

The causes of the Glorious Revolution, 1688

The seven bishops

In 1688, James issued another Declaration of Indulgence and ordered that it be read to congregations in every parish. Seven bishops refused to obey and were arrested, tried and acquitted. When James's wife gave birth to a son two days later, the prospect of a Catholic heir became a reality as James's older children were both daughters.

The collapse of royal power

Invitation to William

Seven leading political figures – both Whig and Tory – signed a letter in the summer of 1688 inviting William of Orange to intervene in England with an armed force. They viewed William as the legitimate heir to the throne because he was married to James's Protestant daughter, Mary. William accepted this invitation for two reasons.

- Those who signed the letter represented both sides of the political elite in England. They consisted of five Whigs and two Tories, and the Earl of Shrewsbury had been raised a Catholic before being persuaded to convert to Anglicanism. The letter stated that '19 parts of 20' in the nation desired change and this was more than enough encouragement for William to launch an invasion that he had already been considering for many months.
- William had been involved in founding the League of Augsburg with a number of other European nations in 1686 in order to restrict Louis XIV's France. The ensuing Nine Years' War (1688–97) became the central focus of William's political and military career and he knew that if he could bring England into the war, the balance of resources that had always favoured France would be tipped against Louis.

The invasion

William was well supplied, with over 500 ships and 21,000 men, and he eventually landed at Torbay after a series of delays in November 1688. His victory was not guaranteed, however, as James had an effective army at his disposal. James amassed his forces on Salisbury Plain, but realising that his hastily assembled troops were inferior in both experience and equipment, he retreated and gave William a clear path to London.

James leaves the throne vacant?

William's forces marched towards London in December and with supporters deserting him in large numbers, James attempted to flee to exile in France, but was captured in Kent and brought to London. Knowing that a drawn-out trial and execution might make a martyr out of James, William allowed him to escape and he joined the court of Louis XIV.

William's supporters could now claim that by fleeing, James had abdicated his throne and the office of monarch had become vacant, thus legitimising William's claim to rule. This version of events was taken up by Whig historians in the 18th and 19th centuries, but has been questioned by others who see the Revolution as a Dutch invasion.

Mind map

Use the information on the opposite page to add detail to the mind map below to help understand the causes of the Glorious Revolution.

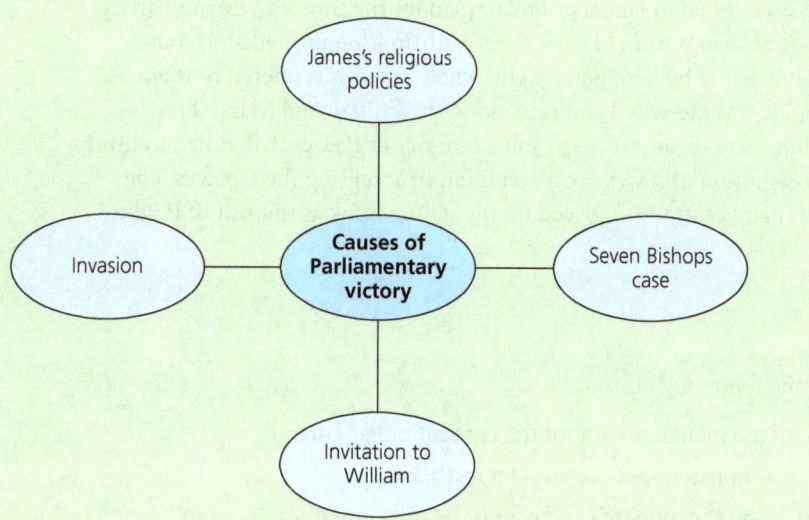

 ## RAG – Rate the interpretation

Read the following interpretation in Extract A.

Shade the sections you agree with in green.

Shade anything you disagree within red.

Shade anything you partly agree/disagree with in amber.

EXTRACT A

From G.M. Trevelyan, England under the Stuarts *(1904).*

The landing of the Prince [William] with a force that could not instantly be overpowered, among a people so well prepared to receive him, made it certain that a free Parliament must be called. But whether that Parliament was to be called under the auspices of James or of William, it was still in the power of James to decide. Fortunately, while he was as strongly determined as his father never to be a constitutional King, and never to give up the interests of his religion, he had not his father's patience to play off armed enemies against each other by deceptive promises and intrigues... Within a month of the landing at Torbay, James was, from a military point of view, as much at his rival's mercy as Richard II had been at the mercy of Bolingbroke, or Charles I at the mercy of Cromwell... If he had consented to remain in England as constitutional monarch, we could not have obtained that union of parties, and that strong monarchical administration on behalf of national and Parliamentary ideals, on which depended the future progress of England and the immediate salvation of Europe.

Government under William and Mary, 1688–1702

The Convention Parliament

A Convention Parliament was established in January 1689 to plan for the future of the monarchy and the country. The more radical Whigs wanted to declare William king immediately, but others favoured a role for his wife Mary by hereditary right. The Crown was offered to them both, and a Declaration of Rights was presented and read aloud to William and Mary. This document outlined both the injustices of James's reign and a number of clauses that aimed to limit royal power, although their recognition of it was not a condition of accepting the Crown. The Declaration was modified and many of its terms placed on the statute book as the Bill of Rights.

The Bill of Rights, 1689

Main clauses

The Bill of Rights contained the following clauses:

- Laws cannot be suspended by the monarch without the consent of Parliament.
- Money cannot be granted to a monarch without consent of Parliament.
- Subjects have the right to petition the monarch and cannot be prosecuted for doing so.
- A monarch cannot keep a standing army in times of peace without the consent of Parliament.
- Elections ought to be free.
- MPs and Lords should have freedom of speech when they are debating in Parliament.
- Excessive bail should not be sought by the authorities or excessive fines imposed.
- No cruel and unusual punishments should be inflicted.
- Parliaments should be held frequently.

Did the Bill of Rights benefit Crown or Parliament?

The Bill of Rights was important in establishing the rights of Parliament for a number of reasons.

- The prospect of an absolute monarchy was vastly diminished.
- The legal position of the army was made certain.
- There was now no doubt that the monarchs could only achieve success if they worked with Parliament.
- Citizens were given certain rights and protections from arbitrary power that were now enshrined in law.

The Bill of Rights benefited the Crown in the following ways.

- William and Mary accepted the throne without conditions, and were not obliged to respect the clauses in the Declaration of Rights and, by extension, the Bill of Rights.
- The historian Christopher Hill has argued that the Bill of Rights was vague, and references in particular to holding frequent Parliaments could still allow for absolutism to creep in.
- There were no provisions for ensuring that elections were regular or free and made no definition of what 'free' actually meant.
- According to John Morrill, the Bill of Rights did not form a contract between the king and his people, and as it was a statute law, it could be repealed by any future Parliament.
- The monarch was still free to decide matters of war and peace, foreign policy and the choice of royal advisers.

Mutiny Acts

As well as restricting the king's powers through the Bill of Rights, a number of Mutiny Acts were passed from 1689, ensuring that the monarch could not **court martial** soldiers at will without the consent of Parliament. As each Mutiny Act was only valid for a year, the king had no choice but to turn to Parliament regularly for approval.

Develop the detail

Below are a sample A-level exam-style question and a paragraph written in answer to this question. The paragraph contains a limited amount of detail. Annotate the paragraph to add additional detail to the answer.

'Parliamentary power increased dramatically in the years 1660–90.' Assess the validity of this view.

Parliamentary power increased most dramatically under William and Mary as a result of the Bill of Rights. William was unable to ignore Parliament because the Bill of Rights included a number of clauses dictating that elections should be free and regular, and that the monarch cannot suspend laws without the approval of Parliament. However, the monarch was still free to decide matters of war and peace and choose his own advisers.

 Turning assertion into argument **a**

Below are a series of definitions, a sample exam question and two sample conclusions. One of the conclusions achieves a high mark because it contains an argument. The other achieves a lower mark because it contains only description and assertion. Identify which is which. The mark scheme on page 5 will help you.

- **Description:** a detailed account.
- **Assertion:** a statement of fact or an opinion which is not supported by a reason.
- **Reason:** a statement which explains or justifies something.
- **Argument:** an assertion justified with a reason.

'Absolute monarchy and Divine Right rule declined steadily in the years 1678–1702.' Assess the validity of this view.

Conclusion 1

William and Mary came to the throne in 1689 and in the Bill of Rights a number of clauses were included, such as those related to the restrictions of monarchical powers over the army and the law. MPs and Lords were given freedom of speech within Parliament and did not have to fear reprisals if they criticised the king's advisers, which had happened in the past. It also ensured that elections should be held regularly and without interference from the monarch. All this suggests that the power of the monarch was restricted and Divine Right rule and absolute monarchy were no longer part of the political system.

Conclusion 2

As a result of the Glorious Revolution, the concept of absolute monarchy was badly damaged, and this was because an entirely new political regime was now in place. The old regime under James did not have to rely on Parliament and alienated it, but William and Mary were subject to the Bill of Rights to a great extent. There is no question that the notion of divine right had been seriously reduced or even removed completely, because the Bill of Rights set down in statute for the first time that a monarch was unable to exercise arbitrary powers such as the right to punish as they saw fit, previously assumed to be given to them by God.

The religious settlement, 1688–1702

The Toleration Act, 1689

Reasons for passing the Toleration Act

Many of the senior Anglican clergy were concerned with ensuring that worship within the Church of England was not modified and would remain uniform. However, in early 1689, William urged the removal of the Test Act for public office holders and faced some hostility from Anglicans. As William was aware of the need to maintain good relations with all sides of the religious spectrum, he attempted to pursue a middle path and suggested that a Toleration Act be passed but that Anglican demands for uniformity be discussed later in 1689.

The content of the Act

- Dissenters were exempted from punishments if they took the oath of allegiance to the Crown and accepted the 1678 Test Act. This meant that they could not enter public employment without swearing loyalty to the Anglican Church.
- Dissenters were not expected to attend an Anglican church but their meetings were closely monitored and the doors of their meeting houses could not be locked.
- The Act gave special dispensations to certain dissenting groups. Quakers were permitted to declare, rather than swear their loyalty to the Crown, as they did not believe in taking oaths.
- The Act excluded Catholics, non-Trinitarians and Jewish people, and as the Test Act had not been repealed, dissenters could technically not sit in Parliament or hold public office.

The impact of religious toleration

- The number of dissenters certainly increased and there were 400,000 by 1714. This equated to 8 per cent of the population.
- William used his royal authority to influence judges and curb Church interference in the lives of Catholics and dissenting sects not covered by the Act.
- The power of the Church courts was severely restricted by the Act.
- Whigs pushed for Anglican clergy to swear an oath to William and Mary. As they had already sworn allegiance to James, many refused and over 400 priests were deprived of their livings. Those removed from office were replaced by more moderate men that were sympathetic to the Whig cause.
- Because the Test Act, Act of Uniformity and Corporation Act were still in force, those who did not swear allegiance to the Anglican Church could not attend university, work in the legal profession or practise medicine.
- Dissenters were still required to pay Church taxes in the form of tithes, even if they did not attend their local parish church.
- Further Toleration Acts were passed in Ireland and Scotland and these did not give dissenters the opportunity to participate in local or national government.
- In reality, Catholics had little to fear from William as he had entered into an alliance with a number of Catholic powers.

Moving from assertion to argument

Below is a sample A-level exam-style question and a series of assertions. Read the exam question and then add a justification to each of the assertions to turn it into an argument.

'The lives of dissenters became significantly easier in the years 1678–1702.' Assess the validity of this view.

There were positive changes for dissenters under Charles II because

_____

_____

After the Glorious Revolution the lives of dissenters became easier because

_____

_____

The Anglican Church continued to dominate under Charles II in the sense that

_____

_____

In many ways, the Anglican Church remained intact under William III

_____

_____

Develop the detail

Below is a sample A-level exam-question and a paragraph written in answer to this question. The paragraph contains a limited amount of detail. Annotate the paragraph to add additional detail to the answer.

'Monarchs in the years 1672–1702 only offered religious toleration to advance their own power.' Assess the validity of this view.

Between 1672 and 1689 all monarchs (Charles II, James II and William III) attempted to advance some degree of religious toleration. Charles and James both favoured toleration for dissenting groups and Catholics, in part because of their desire to establish an absolutist and continental style of government. This is why they both presented Declarations of Indulgence. William, too, was only interested in keeping all sides happy so he could use England to fund his war with France.

The financial settlement

The financial impact of the Nine Years' War

As William brought England into the Nine Years' War on the side of the Dutch, spending increased drastically. Average annual expenditure on the war was £5.4 million. However, the average tax revenue was just £3.6 million.

The revolution in Crown finances

To pay for the war, a land tax was introduced in 1692 and yielded £1 million in its first year. New taxes were also introduced on imported items such as tea, tobacco and alcohol. This was still not enough to meet the shortfall in funding for the war, so the Crown resorted to taking out long-term loans from merchants and City traders and paying them back with interest.

- In 1693, William received a loan from investors of £108,000, and paid the loan back at an interest rate of 10 per cent.
- Other loans were arranged in 1694, and in 1697 a 'malt lottery' was created, whereby benefits were paid to investors from excise taxes on malt.
- The Bank of England was set up in 1694. This was not a bank in the modern sense but a vehicle to secure loans for William. Investors in the Bank were given the authority to deal in bills of exchange, which were given by the Bank as £100 bills. These were effectively bank notes, and in exchange for depositing their money, investors were given proceeds from excise duties.
- This system of public credit led to the creation of the national debt, which stood at £16.7 million in 1698. Repayments took up around 30 per cent of the Crown's annual revenue.

The Civil List

The Civil List Act was passed in 1698, giving William a fixed income of £700,000 per year to meet the expenses of his government, including the salaries of civil servants and judges, as well meeting the expenditure of the royal household. King and Parliament had to meet regularly in order to renew the Civil List for the following year.

Parliamentary control of finance

Concerns among MPs about the huge sums of money being spent on war led to a number of parliamentary commissions being set up.

- In 1690, William agreed to the Public Accounts Act and the first commissions were set up in 1691.
- The commissions were the forerunner to modern-day select committees within Parliament.
- They had the power to interrogate ministers and call for papers from government.
- The commissioners published reports which could expose corruption and waste at William's court.
- The scrutiny was carried out with unprecedented attention to detail. Meetings took place daily and interviews were regularly carried out, although government officials would often obstruct the process.
- The commissions became increasingly used to attack unpopular government ministers in the second half of the 1690s, and high-profile MPs, such as the Speaker, Sir John Trevor, were expelled for financial malpractice.
- The commissions were renewed each year until 1697, when William blocked more from being established.

Simple essay style

Below is a sample exam question. Use your own knowledge and the information on the opposite page to produce a plan for this question. Choose four general points, and provide three pieces of specific information to support each general point. Once you have planned your essay, write the introduction and conclusion for the essay. The introduction should list the points to be discussed in the essay. The conclusion should summarise the key points and justify which point was the most important.

'Financial problems undermined the power of the monarchy in the years 1685–1702.' Assess the validity of this view.

 Analysing interpretations

Study the arguments in the two extracts, and use your contextual knowledge to decide how convincing they are.

You could shade the sections of each extract that you agree with.

Then set out the plan of answer identifying convincing arguments and unconvincing arguments, using your contextual knowledge.

Extract	Arguments you find convincing	Supporting evidence	Arguments you do not find convincing	Supporting evidence
A				
B				

EXTRACT A

From M. Ashley, England in the Seventeenth Century *(1967).*

The loan from the Bank of England [to William] did not have ever to be fully repaid so long as the interest was forthcoming, and thus is the origin of the present funded national debt. In 1698 a new East India Company was founded with statutory privileges in rivalry to the old East India Company which had existed since the days of Queen Elizabeth, and this also undertook to lend the Government money at 8 per cent. Both these institutions were in fact Whig finance companies, and by persuading people to invest in them they not only helped King William III to make war, but also ensured the permanence of the revolution of 1688. Finally, since the Bank and the new East India Company owed their powers to parliament and might not lend to the Crown without parliament's consent, the hold of the Commons upon the Crown was sensibly strengthened.

EXTRACT B

From J. Israel, The Anglo Dutch Moment: Essays on the Glorious Revolution and its World Impact *(2008).*

During the 1690s, this so-called 'Financial Revolution' made a considerable contribution to the emergence of England as a major European power. None of this is controversial. But the fact that these developments grew out of England's new role as a commercial power, committed to a large-scale war effort, has been cited by 'revisionist' historians to suggest that they were therefore merely a by-product of the Glorious Revolution and not integral to it. It is a mistake that stems from viewing Parliament as the main, or sole, author of the Revolution.

The emergence of Whigs and Tories

The importance of the parties

On becoming king, William immediately formed a Privy Council of his own choosing, although he was cautious and included a balance of Whigs and Tories.

The Parliament of 1690 consisted of 225 Whigs and 206 Tories. When he left England to fight against James at the Battle of the Boyne, William showed his preference by leaving a number of loyal Court Tories in charge. Whig rebels attempted to push through a triennial bill in order to ensure regular Parliaments. This was passed by both Houses and William was forced to use his royal veto to block it from becoming law.

The Whig Junto

A group of Whig rebels known as the 'Whig Junto' became influential in 1692 and developed considerable influence in government between 1694 and 1699. They favoured war with France in order to promote the Protestant cause in Europe. Their members included Edward Russell, John Somers, Thomas Wharton and Charles Montagu.

The Triennial Act, 1694

By 1694, the Whig Junto was beginning to dominate government, and its members were given high-profile roles. A second triennial bill was given the royal assent in January 1694 and this new Triennial Act stated that a Parliament could not last longer than three years. This meant that general elections would be held more frequently. The rivalry between Whigs and Tories was stronger than ever but the Act also gave the Commons a new-found confidence. The years after the passing of the Triennial Act can be summarised as follows:

- In 1695, another election was held and the Whigs performed well, cementing their dominance over both Parliament and the Privy Council.
- In 1696, a plot was discovered to assassinate William. The Whigs became more united than ever and William became more reliant on the Whig Junto in the Privy Council. Both Houses adopted a Whig proposal acknowledging William in a loyal 'Association', signed by most MPs.
- In 1697, the opposition to the now-dominant Whig Junto passed a vote limiting William's army to 10,000 men.
- In 1698, the Whig Junto began to collapse. Their opposition was able to secure a bill that reduced William's army further to 7,000, and members of the Junto were promoted or resigned.
- In 1699, a commission investigating confiscated lands in Ireland issued a report and found that William had made excessive grants to loyal courtiers. Parliament passed a bill of resumption, stating that any grants in Ireland given to members of the Privy Council were illegal.
- In the election of 1701, the Tories made gains and began impeachment proceedings against leading Whig Junto members Somers, Montagu and Russell, although they were eventually acquitted by their fellow parliamentarians.

Support or challenge?

Below is a sample A-level exam-style question which asks how far you agree with a specific statement. Below this are a series of events which are relevant to the question. Using your own knowledge and the information on the opposite page decide whether these statements support or challenge the statement in the question.

'A parliamentary monarchy was developed in the years 1678–1702.' Assess the validity of this view.

STATEMENT	SUPPORT	CHALLENGE
The Popish Plot, 1678		
The Exclusion Crisis, 1679–81		
James I's 1685 Parliament		
Bill of Rights, 1689		
Triennial Act, 1694		
Bill of Resumption, 1699		

Complete the paragraph

Below are a sample exam question and a paragraph written in answer to this question. The paragraph contains a point and specific examples, but lacks a concluding analytical link back to the question. Complete the paragraph adding this link back to the question in the space provided.

'The passing of the Triennial Act was the most important reason for increasing parliamentary power in the years 1688–1702.' Assess the validity of this view.

The Triennial Act was vital in expanding parliamentary power because it meant that Parliament could not be ignored and therefore they were able to scrutinise William's government. The Act stated that Parliament should not last longer than three years, and this meant that elections were called regularly. This was positive because it meant that William struggled to form a court party in the House of Commons. It also meant, however, that William's Privy Council became more important than ever to him and he put a lot of power in the hands of the Whig Junto.

_____

_____

4 The establishment of a constitutional monarchy, 1678–1702

The Act of Settlement and the condition of the monarchy and the Church of England in 1702

REVISED

Act of Settlement

The Hanoverian succession

The final major piece of constitutional legislation passed during William's reign was the Act of Settlement of 1701. It stated that future succession would be vested in the House of Hanover, a German royal dynasty, to avoid potential Catholic heirs to the throne. Sophia, the granddaughter of James I, was married to Ernst Augustus, Elector of Hanover, and when she died the succession was passed to her son, George I.

The terms of the Act

- Catholics, and those married to Catholics, were barred from the succession.
- All future monarchs were required to be members of the Church of England.
- Judges could no longer be dismissed without the consent of Parliament.
- Royal pardons were declared void in cases of impeachment.

Some of the clauses were clearly aimed at restricting William's power specifically:

- The monarch was unable to leave Britain without the consent of Parliament.
- The clause that stated that royal pardons were irrelevant in cases of impeachment was only included because the Tories hoped to impeach William's Whig advisers.
- The clause concerning the religion of the monarch reflected concerns over William's Calvinism as much as fear of Catholicism.
- No future monarch was allowed to enter England into a war in order to defend the monarch's home country without the consent of Parliament, which served as a clear response to the risk of appointing a foreign monarch..
- No foreign-born man was allowed to join the Privy Council, sit in either House of Parliament, have a military command or be granted land and titles.

Condition of the monarchy in 1702

The Rage of Party

The period from c1690 to 1715 has been referred to by historians as the Rage of Party, characterised by the instability caused by frequent elections. With more regular elections came a renewed interest in politics from those outside the immediate Political Nation and the electorate were better informed than they had ever been as a result of the lapsing of the Licensing Act of 1695.

How far did Parliament and monarchy become partners?

There are a number of arguments to suggest that monarchy and Parliament did become partners in government.

- William needed parliamentary taxes in order to fight the French and this resulted in Parliament gaining increased control over government finance.
- The Triennial Act made Parliament an institution William could not ignore.
- William was forced to appoint men he loathed to senior positions as a result of parliamentary pressure.
- William was forced to reduce the size of the army as a result of a parliamentary decision.
- The Bill of Rights stated that parliamentary approval needed to be sought for the approval of a standing army in peacetime and outlawed taxation without parliamentary consent.

Although Parliament had become an integral part of the political system, much power was still in the hands of the monarch.

- There was still a desire among many of the political class to join the royal court, particularly as a result of the uncertainty caused by regular elections.
- Much of the royal prerogative was left intact, such as the monarch's power to declare war, dissolve Parliament and veto legislation.
- William had more financial independence than previous monarchs because of the financial revolution and the establishment of a system of long-term borrowing.

🔆 RAG – Rate the timeline

Below is a sample exam-style question and a timeline. Read the question, study the timeline and using three coloured pens, put a red, amber or green star next to the events to show:

Red: events and policies that have no relevance to the question

Amber: events and policies that have some significance to the question

Green: events and policies that are directly relevant to the question

'There was a financial revolution in the years 1688–1702.' Assess the validity of this view.

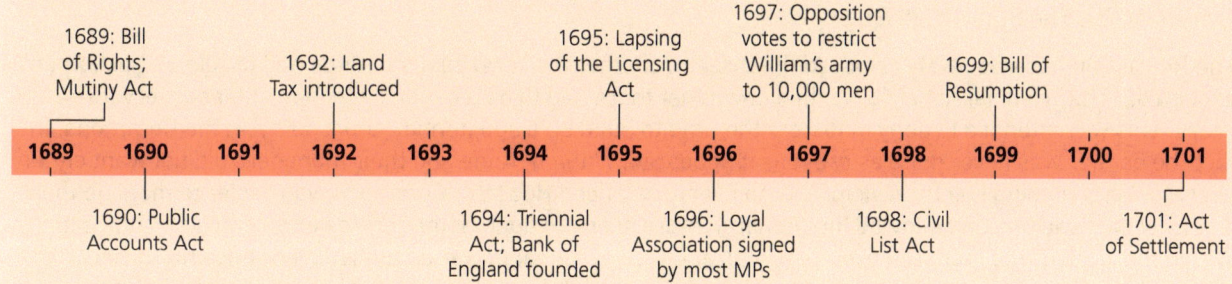

Now repeat the activity with the following question:

To what extent did the power of the monarchy increase in the years 1685–1702?

🔆 Spectrum of importance

Below is a sample exam question and a list of events which could be used to answer the question. Use your own knowledge and the information on the opposite page to reach a judgement about the importance of these general points to the question posed. Write numbers on the spectrum below to indicate their relative importance. Having done this, write a brief justification of your placement, explaining why some of these factors are more important than others. The resulting diagram could form the basis of an essay plan.

'Parliament became a partner in government in the years 1688–1702.' How far do you agree with this view?

1 Bill of Rights
2 Act of Settlement
3 Triennial Act
4 Influence of the Whig Junto
5 Creation of Bank of England
6 Mutiny Acts

Least important ⟷ Most important

Exam focus (A-level)

Below is a sample Level 5 answer to an A-level style question on interpretations. Read it and the comments around it.

Using your understanding of the historical context, assess how convincing the arguments in Extracts A, B and C are in relation to the power of monarchy and Parliament after the Glorious Revolution.

EXTRACT A

From J. Miller, The Stuarts *(2006).*

The Revolution had effectively removed the threat from the royal prerogative. Kings had to rule as Parliament expected... The Triennial Act of 1694... laid down that there had to be a general election at least every three years. This was intended to deny ministers the time to build up a substantial 'court party' in the Commons. In fact the danger was never quite as great as it appeared. William, Anne and their managers did not want either party to win sweeping electoral victories. An evenly balanced House of Commons was easier to manage than a heavily partisan one and allowed the monarch more scope to appoint moderates and neutrals to office... Within the 'crown', the monarch exercised less and less personal power as ministers ruled in his or her name. These ministers derived their power over the monarch from their ability to push government bills (especially money bills) through Parliament, but also from the support that they enjoyed in the wider society.

EXTRACT B

From M. Kishlansky, Monarchy Transformed: Britain 1603–1714 *(1996).*

Parliament established the contractual nature of royal government in the Act of Succession [Settlement], which not only specified the line of descent but attempted to restrict the prerogatives of William's Hanoverian heirs... Whatever their origins, political parties took shape in the reign of William III, when Whigs and Tories battled each other for power and influence. If the purse was the level by which Parliament controlled the King, party was the lever by which the King controlled Parliament. The usefulness of ministers and ministries was in direct proportion to their ability to pass William's programmes. His willingness to discard one party in favour of the other – though he personally decried party division – effectively controlled both parties and restrained parliamentary independence.

EXTRACT C

From G.E. Aylmer, The Struggle for the Constitution *(1963).*

The royal right to suspend legislation was abolished, and the right to dispense with it in particular cases so narrowly restricted as virtually to be taken away. In the revised Coronation Oath the new sovereigns also had to swear to observe parliamentary statutes, another innovation... The illegality of any non-parliamentary taxation was reaffirmed; here James had been infringing various statutes by the autumn of 1688... The legal basis of military discipline was unclear, and this resulted in the passing of an annual Mutiny Act; in this way parliament kept some control over the Army. Moreover because the country became involved in a major European war, the new King came to be completely dependent on parliament for extra taxes, to sustain the military effort.

Historians have long debated the nature of the Glorious Revolution settlement, with some arguing that it represented a genuine revolution in parliamentary government and others interpreting the events as changing nothing except the line of succession. It seems that the argument contained in Extract A is very convincing, because it suggests that the powers of the monarch were changed permanently, but that they were still able to wield an exceptional amount of power. Extract B overstates the argument that the monarch was able to restrain Parliament, and Extract C gives too much weight to the view that Parliament became dominant.

The introductory paragraph sets the tone for the rest of the essay by giving an opinion on the relative strengths of each argument.

The argument in Extract A is strong because it represents clearly the balance of power between monarch and Parliament. It states that the revolution had 'removed the threat of the royal prerogative', and the evidence points towards this being at least partially true. The Bill of Rights of 1689 contained a number of clauses that restricted the power of the monarch. He was unable to levy taxes without Parliament's consent, could not raise a standing army in peacetime without their approval and could not use cruel and unusual punishments. The Triennial Act, mentioned in Extract A when it states that there 'had to be a general election at least every three years', was also important in promoting parliamentary power as the party system was strengthened. The period known as the 'Rage of Party' followed the passing of the Act, and Whigs and Tories jostled for power. The author is correct, however, to argue that it actually caused a reduction in Parliament's power as ministers were 'able to push government bills through Parliament'. This is evident in the rise of the Whig Junto, who William had to rely on to advance his political agenda. The Extract is not without its faults, as it does fail to acknowledge the true extent of prerogative power, as the monarch retained many powers such as the right to declare war and sign peace treaties.

> This paragraph demonstrates a good balance of contextual knowledge and the identification of arguments from the text.

If Extract A focuses on the changes to the royal prerogative as a result of the Glorious Revolution, Extract B outlines the unrivalled power that William had over Parliament. It states that government was now of a 'contractual nature', which alludes to the Bill of Rights, but also that 'party was the lever by which the king controlled Parliament'. This is accurate because the Triennial Act meant that a Parliament could not last longer than three years, and this caused chaos among the Political Nation. In this context, politicians knew that if they wanted to be successful, joining William's court was the preferable option. The most obvious example of this taking place is in the rise of the Whig Junto. The Extract states that William would 'disregard one party in favour of the other', and this was certainly true in the 1690s. In 1690 he left a group of loyal court Tories in charge when he fought the Battle of the Boyne, only to adopt Whig proposals a few years later and use the Whig Junto a lot more. The Tories appeared to be advancing once again in the late 1690s when the Whig Junto fell into decline. The Extract fails, however, to acknowledge that ultimately it was the Whigs that were more influential in the period, for example, their ideas dominated the Glorious Revolution settlement in the first place. On balance, Extract B is therefore limited in gaining a complete insight into the power of king and Parliament.

> This paragraph tackles Extract B, and provides a balanced view of its relative strengths and weaknesses.

Extract C is flawed because it over-emphasises the power that Parliament had as a result of the Glorious Revolution. It alludes to many of the same clauses from the Bill of Rights that the other Extracts do, including stating that 'the illegality of any non-parliamentary taxation was reaffirmed'. There is much evidence to support this, as Parliament had much power of the king's finances. This was demonstrated in the passing of the Civil List Act, which gave the monarch an annual fund of £700,000 for royal expenditure, and Parliament's agreement to taxes such as the Land Tax. However, it could be argued that William was hugely independent financially, as he had access to long-term loans through the Bank of England, lotteries and incorporating shareholders into the East India Company. This gave him enough money to fight the Nine Years' War. The Extract also states the monarch was limited because of the need to pass 'an annual Mutiny Act'. This did force Parliament and monarch to work together regularly, but, crucially, the Extract does not reference just how much power William continued to wield. He had an army in Holland that Parliament had no control over, and he made all strategic decisions in the Nine Years' War.

> This paragraph is critical of the evidence in Extract C and uses detailed and relevant knowledge to assist in the argument.

An excellent answer: each Extract is carefully evaluated to test its strengths and weaknesses. Knowledge of the historical context is used appropriately. This is a Level 5 response, although it could be improved by challenging Extract A further.

Glossary

Anglicised People from other countries (e.g. Scots) who had effectively become English as a result of living in England for a long period of time.

Arminian A follower of the Dutch theologian Jacobus Arminius. Arminians were associated with 'high-church' practices (similar to those of the Catholic Church) such as the use of organs, hymns and bowing to the cross.

Baptists A protestant group that advocates adult baptism.

Biennial Every two years.

Calvinist A follower of the theologian John Calvin. A core belief of Calvinists is that of predestination, whereby every soul's place in heaven or hell is predetermined before they are born.

Court martial A court for trying members of the armed forces.

Dissenters People whose religious beliefs contradict those of the national Church.

Divine Right of Kings The belief that the power of monarchs is God-given.

Enclosure The fencing off of land for the sole use of one owner. This would often lead to a loss of common land where commoners could graze livestock or collect firewood.

Excise tax Tax paid when purchases are made on certain goods.

Favourites A member of the royal court given preference over others.

Feudal dues A tax paid from a lower class to a higher class.

Gentry The class immediately below the nobility. They were wealthy primarily because they owned land.

Habeas Corpus A demand made by a prisoner to their custodian. When issued, the prisoner has the right to go before a court and demand to know the reason for being detained.

Impeachment A process whereby government advisers and officers could be accused of crimes in the House of Commons and tried in the House of Lords.

Justices of the Peace Low-ranking local magistrates.

Liturgy A fixed set of ceremonies, words or phrases used during worship.

Martial law The suspension of ordinary laws in place of military rule.

Millenarian Someone who believes that the second coming of Christ is near. Millenarians believe that this will lead to the establishment of the Kingdom of God on earth.

Monopolies The exclusive right to provide a product or service, given by the monarch.

Nobility A member of the aristocracy, or the highest social class.

Non-Trinitarians Christians who reject the notion of the Holy Trinity – the idea that God, Jesus and the Holy Spirit should have equal status within the Church.

Patronage The power to control appointments to office.

Prerogative The traditional powers of the monarch, such as the power to declare war and appoint advisers to the Privy Council.

Presbyterian A Church governed by a council of elders rather than a hierarchy of bishops.

Privy Council A body of advisers appointed by the monarch.

Puritans Protestants who believed that the Reformation of the Church under Elizabeth I had not gone far enough, and sought to simplify worship and 'purify' it.

Purveyance The Crown's right to purchase goods at a reduced rate in order to sell them for a profit.

Quakers Members of the Religious Society of Friends who believe in the role of Christ's 'Inner Light' in every person. They reject traditional forms of worship.

Reformation The movement to reform the Catholic Church.

Royal absolutism The wielding of absolute, or unrestrained, power by a monarch.

Royal court The family, advisers and extended household of a monarch.

Star Chamber A court made up of Privy Councillors and judges that became infamous for its severe punishments.

Thirty Years' War A war that took place between 1618 and 1648, primarily focused in central Europe. The war was rooted in rivalries between Catholic and Protestant powers.

Tithes A tax, normally levied at one-tenth of a person's income, in order to pay for the upkeep of a parish church.

Tonnage and Poundage Customs duties traditionally granted to the monarch by Parliament. From 1414 they were usually granted for life to each successive king.

United Provinces A Dutch republic formed when seven provinces separated from Spanish rule.

Wardship Charles sold the rights to the guardianship of 'wards', or those in the care of the state that had not come of age. This often proved lucrative to the buyer as they also purchased the rights to use any property that would be inherited by the ward.

Whigs Members of Parliament who were suspicious of both absolutism and Catholicism and resisted Charles II's attempts to maintain his brother, James, in the succession.

Key figures

Charles I (1600–49) King of England, Scotland and Ireland from 1625 until his death in 1649. Born in Scotland to James I and Anne of Denmark, Charles unexpectedly became heir when his older brother, Henry, died. After fighting the First Civil War against Parliament, Charles was a prisoner from 1646 until his execution in January 1649.

Oliver Cromwell (1599–1658) A member of minor gentry family from The Fens of East Anglia, Cromwell rose to become first a town councillor, then an MP and military commander. Proclaimed Lord Protector in 1653, he was briefly succeeded by his son, Richard.

Thomas Fairfax (1612–71) General and Commander-in-Chief of the New Model Army from 1645. Fairfax was not interested in politics and did not take part in the trial of Charles I. He became an MP in the 1650s but avoided the limelight as much as possible.

John Hampden (1595–1643) A Buckinghamshire Puritan and gentleman who gained notoriety for opposing Ship Money in 1636. He became active in the Long Parliament and took up arms at the outbreak of the First Civil War, but was killed early in the conflict.

Denzil Holles (1599–1680) An opponent of the arbitrary government of the 1630s, Holles was one of the Five Members who Charles attempted to arrest in 1642. He became a leader of the Presbyterian faction during the Civil War and was one of the 11 MPs excluded by the Army in 1647.

Henry Ireton (1611–51) Cromwell's son-in-law, Ireton trained as a lawyer in the late 1620s and became a senior commander in the New Model Army. A leading member of the Independent faction, Ireton spoke for the cause of moderation at the Putney Debates.

James I (1566–1625) King of England, Scotland and Ireland from 1603. James became King of Scotland at the age of 13 months after his mother, Mary Queen of Scots, was forced to abdicate. He became King

of England when he succeeded the childless Queen Elizabeth in 1603 as the closest heir. The period of his rule is known as the Jacobean era.

James II (1633–1701) King from 1685 to 1688. James was the second surviving son of Charles I and, despite his conversion to Catholicism, was the legitimate heir to the throne when Charles II died in 1685. His short reign was scarred by suspicion of his religious beliefs and conflicts with the Protestant Political Nation.

William Laud (1573–1645) Laud was a well-known Arminian and became Archbishop of Canterbury in 1633 and was responsible for implementing Charles's religious policy. He was impeached in 1641 and executed in 1645.

John Lilburne (1614–57) Lilburne was involved in Puritan pamphleteering from the 1630s and enlisted as a captain in the parliamentary Army. He became a Leveller towards the end of the Civil War. He was imprisoned by Parliament several times and was involved in writing *An Agreement of the People*.

Henrietta Maria (1609–69) The daughter of Henry IV of France, Henrietta married Charles in 1625. Unpopular because of her Catholic faith, she was forced to seek refuge in France at the height of the Civil War in 1644. She was the mother of two future monarchs: Charles II and James II.

George Monck (1608–70) Monck was from a Devon gentry family and became a professional soldier at a young age. He fought for Charles in the First Civil War and later for Cromwell in the Third Civil War. He became Commander-in-Chief of the republican forces in Scotland, and from here he plotted the restoration of the Rump Parliament.

Titus Oates (1649–1705) After performing poorly at Cambridge, Oates become a priest in the Church of England and later worked as a navy chaplain but was dismissed. He converted to Catholicism in 1677 and enrolled at a Jesuit college for priests in France, only to be thrown out within months. After fabricating the Popish Plot and enjoying fame for a time, he was imprisoned, only to be released after the Glorious Revolution.

Thomas Osborne, Earl of Danby (1632–1712)
Danby became a Privy Councillor in 1673 and assisted in arranging the marriage of William and Mary in 1677. He encouraged Charles II to pursue a pro-Dutch policy after years of alliance with Louis XIV. He was part of the group of seven that invited William of Orange to become monarch in 1688.

John Pym (1584–1643)
Trained as a lawyer, Pym became a leading critic of Charles and the effective leader of the opposition to Charles in the Long Parliament. He was responsible for the Grand Remonstrance the Solemn League and Covenant with the Scots.

Prince Rupert (1619–82)
Rupert was Charles's nephew and had gained experience of fighting in the Thirty Years' War. At just 23 he was appointed commander of the Royalist cavalry and was exiled from England towards the end of the Civil War. In later life he returned to England and became a naval commander.

James Scott, 1st Duke of Monmouth (1649–85)
The eldest illegitimate son of Charles II, born to his mistress, Lucy Walter. During the Exclusion Crisis, the Whigs claimed that Charles had married Walter, thus giving some legitimacy to Monmouth's claim to the throne. He was executed after the failed Monmouth Rebellion.

George Villiers, Duke of Buckingham (1592–1628)
Villiers was the favourite of James I and became a close adviser to Charles during his early reign. He led a number of failed foreign policy expeditions and was assassinated by a disgruntled sailor in 1628.

Thomas Wentworth, Earl of Strafford (1593–1641)
Although he opposed Charles before personal rule, Wentworth switched sides and became a firm supporter of the monarchy. Appointed President of the Council of the North in 1628, he was sent to Ireland as Lord Deputy in 1632 and executed by the Long Parliament in 1641.

William III (1650–1702)
Stadtholder (leader) of the Dutch Republic as William of Orange from 1672 and King of England, Scotland and Ireland from 1689. His mother, Mary, was a daughter of Charles I and he married his first-cousin, also called Mary, in 1677.

Timeline

1603	Death of Elizabeth I and accession of James I
1604	First Parliament of James's reign called
	Hampton Court Conference
1610	The Great Contract introduced by Cecil
1614	The 'Addled Parliament'
1625	Death of James I and accession of Charles I
	Charles marries Henrietta Maria
	Attack on Cadiz
1626	Forced loan
1627	Five Knights' Case
	Attack on La Rochelle
	Archbishop Abbot suspended for refusing to approve an Arminian sermon
1628	Petition of Right
	Assassination of Buckingham
1629	Three Resolutions
	Beginning of personal rule
1632	Wentworth sent to Ireland as Lord Deputy
1633	Laud appointed Archbishop of Canterbury
1634	William Noy appointed Attorney General
1636	The Book of Canons sent to the Scottish clergy
1637	The English Prayer Book sent to Scottish churches

	The trial of Bastwick, Burton and Prynne
	Hampden's Ship Money case
1638	National Covenant founded
1639	Taxpayers' strike
	First Bishops' War
1640	Short Parliament assembled
	Second Bishops' War
	Long Parliament assembled
	Root and Branch Petition
1641	Triennial Act
	Execution of Strafford
	Irish Rebellion
	Grand Remonstrance
1642	Five Members Incident
	Militia Ordinance
	Charles fails to seize Hull
	Nineteen Propositions
	Declaration of war
	Battle of Edgehill
1643	Solemn League and Covenant
	Death of John Pym
1644	Battle of Marston Moor

Quick quizzes at www.hoddereducation.co.uk/myrevisionnotes

1645	Self Denying Ordinance	**1659**	Monck restores the Rump
	Formation of the New Model Army	**1660**	Declaration of Breda
	Battle of Naseby		Restoration of Charles II
1646	Charles surrenders to the Scots	**1661**	Venner's Rising
	Newcastle Propositions		Corporation Act
1647	The Scots leave England	**1662**	Hearth Tax introduced
	The New Model Army begins to elect Agitators		Act of Uniformity
	Seizure of Charles and Army revolt		Declaration of Indulgence
	Heads of the Proposals	**1664**	Triennial Act
	Putney Debates		Conventicle Act
	Charles escapes from Hampton Court	**1665**	Five Mile Act
	The Engagement with the Scots		Second Anglo-Dutch War begins
1648	Vote of No Addresses	**1668**	James converts to Catholicism
	Second Civil War	**1670**	Treaty of Dover
	Windsor Prayer Meeting		Second Conventicle Act
	Treaty of Newport negotiations	**1672**	Third Anglo-Dutch War
	Pride's Purge		Stop of the Exchequer
1649	Trial and execution of Charles		Declaration of Indulgence
	Invasion of Ireland	**1673**	Test Act
	Levellers suppressed	**1677**	Marriage of William and Mary
1650	Toleration Act	**1678**	Popish Plot
	Blasphemy Act	**1679**	Beginning of Exclusion Crisis
	Battle of Dunbar	**1683**	Rye House Plot
1651	Navigation Act	**1685**	Death of Charles II
	Battle of Worcester		Monmouth Rebellion
1652	Anglo-Dutch War	**1686**	*Godden v. Hales*
1653	Cromwell closes down the Rump Parliament	**1687**	Declaration of Indulgence
	Parliament of Saints	**1688**	Glorious Revolution
	Instrument of Government and beginning of the Protectorate	**1689**	Bill of Rights
			Toleration Act
1655	Penruddock's Rising	**1690**	Public Accounts Act
	Rule of the Major Generals	**1694**	Triennial Act
1656	James Nayler Case		Bank of England founded
1657	Humble Petition and Advice	**1698**	Civil List Act
1658	Death of Cromwell	**1701**	Act of Settlement
	Accession of Richard Cromwell as Lord Protector	**1702**	Death of William III